POETS IN BRIEF

GEORGE CRABBE

POETS IN BRIEF

LONDON
Cambridge University Press
FETTER LANE

NEW YORK · TORONTO
BOMBAY · CALCUTTA · MADRAS
Macmillan

TOKYO
Maruzen Company Ltd

GEORGE CRABBE

An Anthology

Chosen by

F. L. LUCAS

Fellow of King's College
Cambridge

CAMBRIDGE

AT THE UNIVERSITY PRESS

1933

To

ROGER FRY

CONTENTS

vii

INTRODUCTION[1]

IT is extraordinary what prosaic people poets can be; or, if you like, what prosaic people can be poets. This paradox has long become a platitude; yet there are moments when it can still make us rub astonished eyes. We may remind ourselves that even Byron is most unlikely to be pacing his chamber in the throes of *Manfred* the morning we meet him; as Byron himself said, 'I never can get people to understand that poetry is the expression of excited emotion, and that there is no such thing as a life of passion any more than a continual earthquake....Besides, who would ever shave themselves in such a state?' It is obvious; and yet we can sympathize so well with Mr Coolidge of Boston in his ill-concealed disappointment at the author of *Childe Harold*—'having expected to meet a misanthropical gentleman in wolfskin breeches, answering in fierce monosyllables, instead of a man of this world'. Yet, in fact, few poets have lived their part as romantically as Byron; shall we ever grow used to the far wider contrast between *Tintern Abbey* and the humdrum, horse-faced personage who wrote it, between *The Ancient Mariner* and the flaccid, snub-nosed countenance of Coleridge?

There is often an equally incongruous contrast between peoples or landscapes and the literature they produce. How much more poetry the reader of history might naturally expect from the country of François I and Bayard, of Napoleon I and Napoleon III, than from the country of Henry VIII and Oliver Cromwell, of George IV and Queen Victoria! No doubt such generalizations are too easy: by

[1] This originally appeared as an article in *Life and Letters*.

choosing one's examples tactfully one can prove almost anything. Matthew Arnold, discussing in this way the Celtic and Teutonic elements in our literature, reached the most curious conclusions by contrasting, as racially characteristic, the worst doggerel he could find on an English tombstone with some elaborate triad from early Welsh poetry. Still, it is surely not too rash to say that 'John Bull' has always been a far more prosaic, far less passionate and imaginative figure than 'la belle France'; and yet, for some reason, it is from north of the Channel that the richer poetry has come.

Or consider the effect of landscape. To generations the Alps have seemed the embodiment of the sublime and beautiful; few would claim that for London and the Midlands. And yet, name the six chief poets of Switzerland—there, indeed, would be a test of general knowledge. And how many poets have ever lived in the real Arcadia, heart-rendingly beautiful as its mountains remain to this day? Whereas Cambridge, set in the grey sobriety of its fenlands, has, as we all know, been a nest of nightingales for centuries.

Is there some law of reaction to explain this paradox? Is it like the tendency of the dwellers in flat lands, from Babel to Venetia and Flanders, to pile up heaven-piercing towers? Shall we say that, as only the hardiest of plants can survive in a Sahara, so there are no poets so poetic as those born into some Philistia; and retire with a glowing sense of having added to the great store of general truths?

Alas, these are half-truths at best. If the prosaic English have produced great poetry, the prosaic Swiss have not; and if the natural beauty of Switzerland has failed to produce it, what on the other hand of the natural beauty of Greece—which seems so naturally reflected in the beauty of Greek literature? Our generalizations collapse; all except this simple one—that however dull and prosaic a country, a race, or an individual may at first sight seem, we can never be sure that they will not suddenly blossom into poetry. For it is a strange plant, that sows itself in the most unlooked-for places: like an ash-tree springing up on a chimney stack, or a swallow nesting in the cab of a railway engine. Picture, for instance, a human being with not much imagination, not much ear for verbal music, not much passion for the beauty of nature— fonder, by his own admission, of watching faces in the street; in temper a scientist rather than an artist, and indifferent to painting, music, or architecture; preferring 'in botany grasses, the most useful but least ornamental; in minerals, the earths and sands; in entomology, the minuter insects'; and given at one time to roaming the sea-shore (Parnassian occupation!) in search of drowned dogs to dissect. See him, to complete the picture, as by profession an unsuccessful surgeon, then a clergyman of the Church of England noted for his strong sermons against 'enthusiasm'. How many of us would subscribe very hopefully to a forthcoming edition of such a person's poems? Do you ask more details—his origin? He was the child of a tax-collector with mathematical leanings, and of a publican's widow. The surroundings of his childhood? A drab and straggling street, bounded by a monotony of grey shingle and grey sea on one side, on the other by a barren heath and a mud-bound marsh, with dark brown water oozing slowly down its dykes. The society he mixed with—by necessity, if not by choice? The provincials of a petty port; London tradespeople; the stiff correctness of an eighteenth-century ducal castle; or else such country types as these described by his son—'One was a jolly old farmer, with much of the person and humour of Falstaff, a face as rosy as brandy could make it, and an eye teeming with subdued merriment; for he had that prime quality of a joker, superficial gravity: the other was a relative of the family, a wealthy yeoman, middle-aged, thin, and muscular. He was a bachelor, and famed for his indiscriminate attachment to all who bore the name of woman—young or aged, clean or dirty, a lady or a gipsy, it mattered not to him: all were equally admired. He had peopled the village green; and it was remarked, that, whoever was the mother, the children might be recognized in an instant to belong to him. Such was the strength of his constitution, that, though he seldom went to bed sober, he retained a clear eye and a stentorian voice to his eightieth year, and coursed when he was ninety. . . . Another of the sisterhood was Miss Waldron, late of Tamworth—dear, good-humoured, hearty, masculine Miss Waldron, who could sing a jovial song like a fox-hunter, and like him I had almost said toss a glass: and yet there was such an air of high *ton*, and such intellect mingled with these manners, that the perfect lady was not veiled for a moment—no, not when with a face rosy-red, and an eye beaming with mirth, she would seize a cup and sing "Toby Fillpot", glorying as it were in her own jollity'. Here, to be sure, were haunts for Fielding; but hardly for Apollo. And yet after a century crowded with the work of younger writers George Crabbe still keeps his place and his power to please.

No wonder if he was often a prosaic poet: the wonder is that, with such antecedents and surroundings and qualities of mind, he was a poet at all. How prosaic he can be, had better be admitted at once. Those who explore him must be prepared to drop at any moment into abysses of bathos. Again and again he invites that gibe of Alphonse Daudet at some poetaster: 'Ça un poète!—tout au plus de l'infanterie montée':

xii

A quiet, simple man was *Abel Keene*,
He meant no harm, nor did he often mean:
He kept a school of loud rebellious boys,
And growing old, grew nervous with the noise.

The timid girls, half dreading their design,
Dip the small foot in the retarded brine.

And I was thankful for the moral sight,
That soberised the vast and wild delight.

It is as bad as Wordsworth at his worst. Yet there is a great
deal more in Crabbe than doggerel. His poetry and his life
are both alike in this: they seem monotonous and dingy. They
are; but look closer; mixed with their grey texture are threads
of deeper and of brighter colour—flashes of quiet heroism;
sorrows felt passionately, though the words are few; and a
lifelong loyalty to truth, sometimes sad, sometimes sardonic.
Truthfulness—that is Crabbe's master quality, and the secret
of his lasting appeal. He did not deal in beatific visions; he
trailed no clouds of glory; he has no claims to be called 'great'.
But whether it was a dyke of muddy water in a marsh or the
brooding memories of an old woman at her cottage door, he
had no common power of sight, and insight, and of saying
what he saw.

His life, indeed, is very like one of his own tales. Under its
sober surface lies both grimness and romance. Already as he
grew into boyhood his quiet home was darkened by the
sombre rages which began to grow upon his father, to the
point of throwing the crockery about the room, until his wife
came to dread the sound of his returning footsteps. Strange
destinies, too, awaited the poet's younger brothers. The third
son became captain of a slave-ship; one day his black cargo
broke loose, mastered the vessel, and set their white captors
adrift in an open boat; Captain Crabbe and his men were

never heard of more. A younger brother still was captured by the Spaniards, settled in Mexico, and grew rich; his wealth reminded the Church that he was a heretic; he was forced to leave his wife, children, and all he possessed, and flee to Honduras, where he founded, if not a new fortune, at all events a new family. For it appears from the *Belize Advertiser* of January 1840 that, fantastic as it sounds, the author of *The Parish Register* was the probably unsuspecting uncle of a colony of little black Crabbes beyond the Atlantic. His own boyhood was uneventful; but the touch of poetry was already there. His father, though by profession a revenue-collector (like the father of Horace, two thousand years before) and in charge of the salt-duties at Aldborough, had tastes not only for mathematics, but for verse as well, and would read Milton and Young in the evenings to his family; further, he took in *Martin's Philosophical Magazine*, a journal with a Poets' Corner which the father flung aside and the son learnt by heart. This boyish habit has left its mark on that curious poem Crabbe wrote years after, called *The Newspaper*, with its description of such newspaper poets:

> This Poets' Corner is the place they choose,
> A fatal nursery for an infant Muse;
> Unlike that corner where true poets lie,
> These cannot live, and *they* shall never die.

Fortunately, Crabbe's own 'infant Muse' found a healthier nursery than this elsewhere in Aldborough, among its old wives and ancient mariners. From them the future story-teller was already in his boyhood gathering his material:

> They told of days where many goes to one—
> Such days as ours; and how a larger sun,
> Red, but not flaming, roll'd with motion slow,
> On the world's edge, but never dropp'd below.

Nor was it only the old who found in this quiet child a listener:

> There were fond girls that took me to their side
> To tell the story how their lovers died.

In the same way, with the same already eager human interest, he picked acquaintance with lonely shepherds on Aldborough Heath, and with smugglers down the coast. If Crabbe's schooling was scanty and his culture never wide, he early learnt things that books could never have taught him,

> And all that boys acquire whom men neglect.

Next followed apprenticeship to a series of surgeons; a rough experience, apt to include helping the surgeon's plough-boy at odd moments. Then, at seventeen, came romance. He fell in love with Sarah Elmy. The poems he addressed 'To Mira' seem starchy and sickly enough to modern taste; it only shows how rash it is to accuse writers of 'insincerity': seldom has love proved truer. To win her he battled for twelve years against discouragement, poverty, and debt. Twice he tried to make his way in London. His first attempt was in 1776–7, as a surgeon; but he was too poor to pay for proper teaching, and his efforts at self-help led to little result—except that his landlady, finding he had a dead baby in his cupboard, became convinced that he had dug up her William, buried the week before, and was only prevented from haling him to the Mansion House by the production of the child with its face, fortunately, still intact. It is clear that Crabbe was even less made for medicine than Keats; the idea of being called on to do a serious operation was a nightmare to him; and after struggling two years more with his profession at Aldborough he decided to abandon it and take the decisive step, as it proved, of his whole life.

Here again the prose of Crabbe's career is lit up for an instant by a flash of poetry; for this decision was made by him on a gloomy winter's day in 1779, on the bleak Marsh Hill above Aldborough, as he stood and gazed at a muddy pool there, called 'the Leech-pond'. On that spot, with as much 'Resolution and Independence' as Wordsworth's own Leech-gatherer, Crabbe determined to stake all on his poetry. The next April, aged twenty-five, with three pounds in his pocket, he sailed on a smack for London, where, just ten years before him, Chatterton had likewise sought his fortune, and found his fate. Fortunately Chatterton was not even a name to Crabbe until after his arrival there.

In that Purgatory he suffered a whole year. His journal makes moving reading, with its mixture of a simplicity that hopes to conquer the world of letters by means of Epistles to Prince William Henry and Epistles from the Devil, and a courage that refuses to despair at the obdurate deafness of peers and publishers alike, of North and Shelburne, Dodsley and Becket; even when the writer is reduced to fourpence-halfpenny in the world. Only at moments there is wrung from him a cry of wretchedness: 'Oh Sally, how I want you!' Summer came; amid its heats he watched the flames of the Gordon Riots licking up the walls of Newgate; a barren winter followed, then a hopeless spring. A debtors' gaol was gaping for him, when he played his last card and wrote an appeal to Burke. He left it at Burke's door, together with a copy of his poem, *The Library*; then in the anguish of his suspense paced up and down Westminster Bridge (again we think of Wordsworth) all night long. That night the tide had turned.

Struck by the letter (as well he might be), still more by the man himself, Burke took instant action, although himself in the thick of a political crisis. He introduced the young surgeon from Suffolk to the greatest of the day, to Fox, to Reynolds, to Johnson; arranged for the publication of *The Library*; arranged for the ordination of its author and his appointment to a curacy at Aldborough. Then, when Crabbe's native town showed itself ill-disposed to take the returned saltmaster's son for its spiritual shepherd, this ever-patient patron had him made instead chaplain to the Duke of Rutland. Thenceforth Crabbe's long life flowed evenly to its close. *The Village* appeared successfully in 1783; the same year saw him wedded at last to the woman he had toiled so patiently to win. In 1785 followed *The Newspaper*. Then for twenty-two years, from the age of thirty to fifty-one, he published nothing. Glad to escape from his too aristocratic chaplaincy to a country parsonage, he spent his quiet days in botanizing, preaching against the enthusiasm of the Methodists, rearing a family, and delighting its youthful members by making periodical bonfires in his garden of massive manuscripts of verse, to say nothing of three novels—mountains of paper whose bulk, if burnt indoors, would have endangered the house. Sermons he composed with less ardour; in later life, at least, he would preach the same ones at two-year intervals—a characteristically commonsense arrangement. 'As like Parson Adams' (said Lord Chancellor Thurlow) 'as twelve to the dozen', he maintained calm, but firm relations with his parishioners; tithe-days called from him no elaborate ceremony, but a blunt 'I must have some money, gentlemen'. His life makes a sleepy record, even without the opium he took for his digestion in his latter years. And yet under this tranquillity there still lurked deeper feelings—wild impulses like that sudden uncontrollable longing for the sea which made him one day mount his horse, ride sixty miles to the Lincoln coast, enter the waves, and so return; and secret troubles, like the melancholia which attacked his wife at intervals from 1796 till her death in 1813 There is something very pitiful in the words written by him or one of her old letters: 'Nothing can be more sincere than this nothing more reasonable and affectionate; and yet happiness was denied'. And yet a truer epitaph on his long love-story lies, perhaps, in those other lines he wrote on the paper wrapping of his dead wife's wedding-ring, clumsy, yet moving in their sincerity:

> The ring so worn as you behold,
> So thin, so pale, is yet of gold;
> The passion such it was to prove—
> Worn with life's care, love yet was love.

Had Crabbe died at fifty, he would be to-day as obscure a figure as Tickell or Parnell. *Inebriety*, *The Candidate*, *The Library*, *The Newspaper*, and even *The Village* would scarcely have kept his memory alive. But in 1807 this poet of a past age presented himself before the new generation with a volume of poems containing, besides his previous work, *The Parish Register* and *Sir Eustace Grey*. Success encouraged him, and *The Borough* followed in 1810, the *Tales* in 1812, *Tales of the Hall* in 1819. With surprising ease and swiftness this old man, who had been born under George II, established his position as a leading poet in the world of Napoleon and Wellington, Scott and Byron. He made the acquaintance of Scott, Campbell, Rogers, Bowles, Moore, and Wordsworth; he had become rector of comfortable Trowbridge, with his grand-children growing up round him; and yet all was not well. He suffered from being too old, or else not old enough; the lover, long ago, of Sarah Elmy still felt woman's charm; he seemed terribly alone in the bustling streets of his prosperous parish. 'I cannot bear to belong to nobody.' He tried to satisfy himself with feminine friendships, but they had a way of hovering unhappily on the brink of something more. 'I have,' he writes to Mrs Leadbeater, 'though at considerable distances, six female friends, unknown to each other, but all dear, very dear to me.' The distances did not always remain so considerable. In his sixtieth year he was even accepted by one young woman, only to recoil himself on second thoughts. That was unfortunate; but he was needlessly contrite, one feels, at having thereby caused Miss Ridout to reject a young man, who was 'an excellent match in every respect except a certain weakness of intellect'. He did not, however, escape the criticism of others. 'The cake was no doubt very good,' observed one lady, 'but there was too much sugar to cut through in getting at it.' An old squire was blunter: 'Damme, Sir, the very first time Crabbe dined at my house, he made love to my sister'. It is an old story—laurelled age and laughing youth, Corneille and Mademoiselle du Parc, Goethe and Bettina, Ibsen and his Princess of Orangia: it would be very comical if it were not tragic. Yet it is strange to find something so naïve and *doucereux* in Crabbe of all men, 'Nature's sternest painter, yet the best'. So much harder is it to sum up a human being than biographers often suppose. It was no mere softening of old age: the sturdy resolution of forty years before was still his; in 1818, when he supported the unpopular candidate at Trowbridge and a hostile mob threatened to tear his chaise and him to pieces if he went to the poll, the old rector replied that they might kill him if they chose, but while he lived he would vote, and passed through their midst unharmed. A commonsense Liberal to the last, he died on the eve of the Reform Bill in 1832.

Naïve, yet shrewd; straightforward, yet sardonic; blunt, yet tender; quiet, yet passionate; realistic, yet romantic—such was the man, and such is his poetry. The first impression is of a prosaic naturalist, both in the scientific and in the literary sense of that word. He botanizes and entomologizes, so to speak, in his observation of nature and human nature; with a preference for hemlock over roses, for moths over butterflies. He is more interested in a flatworm than a python. He shows the absorption of an eager student of medicine in a really bad case. Hence the familiar phrase about 'Pope in worsted stockings'; hence the complaint of Wordsworth that 'Crabbe's verses are in no sense poetry' and 'nineteen-twentieths of his pictures are mere matters of fact'; of Coleridge, that there was in him 'an absolute defect of the high imagination'; of Landor's Porson that he 'wrote with a twopenny nail . . . on mud walls'.

It is an understandable attitude. Crabbe is more than a verse Defoe, but he is that in part. It is not necessarily a weakness: Crabbe's Romantic contemporaries and successors would have been none the worse if their own pictures had more often been 'matters of fact'. He may lack 'the high imagination', but at least he had, what they often wanted, that lower imagination which can see and make others see, not things that never were, but things that are. Crabbe, indeed, belonged to that class of human beings of whom we may say that pink spectacles make them see red. They would rather face the worst truths than pretty illusions:

> Come, search within, nor sight nor smell regard;
> The true physician walks the foulest ward.

So Crabbe set out to tear the honeysuckle off Goldsmith's Deserted Village.

> Since vice the world subdued, and waters drown'd,
> Auburn and Eden can no more be found.

It was not that Goldsmith had never known hard times himself: he had fiddled his vagabond way across Europe; it was a difference, not of experience, but of temperament. In this reaction against Goldsmith Crabbe first found himself, just as Fielding had begun by loathing and parodying Richardson.

> Then shall I dare these real ills to hide
> In tinsel trappings of poetic pride? . . .
> By such examples taught, I paint the Cot,
> As Truth will paint it, and as Bards will not.

The style is the faded convention of a hundred and fifty years ago; the sentiment might be that of a modern poet rebelling against Tennyson, or against the Georgians. We can understand how Johnson then, and Hardy a century later, felt at once the appeal of a mind so cleared of cant; indeed, I had already found myself wondering whether Crabbe must not have been one of Hardy's favourite poets, even before biography disclosed that from him Hardy derived his own first impulse towards realism. After all, this is an ancient school of writing—older, no doubt, even than the day when the Muses met Hesiod keeping sheep on Mount Helicon and taught him that they could tell truth as well as fiction, and paint life's harsh realities as well as Homer's high romance. Indeed, it is worth opening Crabbe and Hesiod side by side to see how vigorously a certain type of rustic temper can persist across the division of seas and centuries—disillusioned, sharptongued, shrewd-witted, yet with a sense of beauty of its own. The bleak Thracian gale that pipes across Hesiod's Bœotia echoes the north-easter that nips East Anglia; the Greek shrew

> Who, though her wedded husband be a stout man and a sage,
> With never a fire will roast him into a raw old age,

bears a family resemblance, despite three thousand years, to her Suffolk sister:

> Twelve heavy years this patient soul sustain'd
> This wasp's attacks, and then her praise obtain'd,
> Grav'd on a marble tomb, where he at peace remain'd.

Much nearer home, Crabbe invites a more obvious comparison with Cowper: there is the same fondness for quiet English country, the same fondness, alas, for mere prose in metre. As a letter-writer, Cowper must stand far higher: as a poet of landscape, and of human character, he seems to me inferior. He lacked both Crabbe's knowledge and Crabbe's strength; indeed, the mixture in him of maiden lady and hunted sheep, despite all its pathos, ends by tiring the patience. Then there is that other far greater poet of the country and the poor, who in his flights of inspiration soars into heavens far out of sight of Aldborough Heath, but also, when inspiration leaves him, flounders almost lower, even, than Crabbe himself—Wordsworth. Little comparison is possible, but there is one difference of some interest in its effects—the difference between Wordsworth's blank verse and Crabbe's couplet. For grand moments in the grand manner, blank verse is doubtless unsurpassable; but for general purposes it tends to lapse, as Goldsmith already saw before Wordsworth's day or Cowper's, into 'a disgusting solemnity'. With all its faults, the couplet is far less subject to that failing. Crabbe was slovenly. He wrote too fast—six times as fast as Virgil—thirty lines a day. He never learnt what Boileau taught Racine, not only to rhyme, but 'rimer difficilement'. As sure as fate, a 'boy' in Crabbe is doomed, if to no other 'employ', then to a 'hoy'. None the less for his purposes he chose the right measure.

He also learnt, more slowly, to choose the right method for his gifts. It was in vivid and individual detail, not in vague generalizations, that his power lay. The sublime may be vague, as the mountains and the heavens seem but the vaster for mist and cloud; but the village brook, the woodland pool, need clarity to be at their best. From *Libraries* and *Villages* and *Boroughs* he passed more and more to tales of individual lives—from the general to the particular, from the static to the dynamic. Even in his earlier work the most vital passages had been, apart from the landscapes, the sketches of characters like Phœbe Dawson or the Widow Goe; and the later letters of the *Borough* are indistinguishable from the *Tales*.

In these it is not the plots that are striking—they are adequate, seldom more; a village girl is seduced by a footman, a village coquette passes through all the slow stages from ballroom to almshouse, a young man is entrapped by a young minx in a nobleman's household. What remains outstanding is the truth of detail in the characters; especially the pictures of degeneration, 'little by little'—for instance, the prim Parish Clerk, a sort of Malvolio, who stoops in the end to steal from the offertory-bag. Such gradual progresses of a soul, upward or downward, are too long to quote; but Crabbe's gift of catching a situation or a human type in a couplet or so lends itself better to the purpose. There is, for instance, the lovers' quarrel:

> The youth, repulsed, to one more mild convey'd
> His heart, and smil'd on the remorseless maid;
> The maid, remorseless in her pride, the while
> Despis'd the insult and return'd the smile;

or the village gossips:

> Theirs is that art, which English wives alone
> Profess—a boast and privilege their own...
> When they engage the tongue, the eye, the ear,
> Reply when listening, and when speaking, hear;

or the charity-boy in the workhouse:

> There was he pinch'd and pitied, thump'd and fed,
> And duly took his beatings and his bread;

or again, we see the gardener's wife standing proudly upon her privileges:

> 'Why "Lonicera" wilt thou name thy child?'
> I ask'd the Gardener's wife in accents mild.
> 'We have the right', replied the sturdy dame,
> And Lonicera was the infant's name.

Miranda the blue-stocking aspires to mathematics:

> She thought indeed the higher parts sublime;
> But then they took a monstrous deal of time.

The tactful wife leads her husband with a velvet glove:

> She only begg'd to rule in small affairs,
> And ease her wedded lord of common cares,
> Till he at length thought every care was small,
> Beneath his notice, and she had them all.

The toad-eating nephew waits to inherit from his aunt:

> 'They taught you nothing; are you not, at best,'
> Said the proud Dame, 'a trifler and a jest?
> Confess you are a fool!' He bow'd and he confess'd.

> This vex'd him much, but could not always last:
> The dame is buried, and the trial past.

This simple country clergyman, it appears, was something of a wit; at times, a bitter one:

> 'I speak my mind, I love the truth', quoth he;
> Till 'twas his fate that useful truth to find,
> 'Tis sometimes prudent not to speak the mind.

> 'How well my father liv'd!' she says. 'How well,
> My dear, your father's creditors could tell.'

To those who do not know Crabbe intimately, it must always seem most extraordinary that Jane Austen should have said she could imagine herself as Mrs Crabbe.[1] It seems too like a silk-gloved hand clasping a woollen one. And yet, after reading a piece like *Flirtation: A Dialogue*, the wonder is rather where this blunt parson acquired such malicious lightness of touch. This piece is a conversation between a young lady, who has not been precisely a Penelope, and her confidante, pending the return of her betrothed Ulysses; and its disquisition on the Art of Weeping makes a pretty pendant to that on the Art of Swooning or Running Mad in Jane Austen's *Love and Freindship*:

> To touch him nearer, and to hold him fast,
> Have a few tears *in petto* at the last;
> But this with care ! For 'tis a point of doubt,
> If you should end with weeping or without.
> 'Tis true you much affect him by your pain,
> But he may want to prove his power again;
> And then, it spoils the look, and hurts the eyes—
> A girl is never handsome when she cries.
> Take it for granted, in a general way,
> The more you weep for men, the more you may.
> Save your resources; for though now you cry
> With good effect, you may not by and by.
> It is a knack; and there are those that weep
> Without emotion, that a man may sleep;
> Others disgust—'tis genius, not advice,
> That will avail us in a thing so nice.

But, alas, these silken nets are spread in vain—all ends with the arrival of a letter announcing that the errant Ulysses has himself succumbed in marriage to a Circe in Guernsey. It is worth noting what a way the couplet has of begetting wit; imagine the above in blank verse, or recall the mountainous

---

[1] Prof. Elton quotes an amusing passage from one of her letters: 'I have never seen the death of Mrs Crabbe. . . . Poor woman! I will comfort him as well as I can, but I do not undertake to be good to her children . . . she had better not leave any'.

gambols of *The Prelude*. Not that Crabbe cannot be atrocious; only, when a writer shows such conscious humour, it is hard to be sure how far the humour is unconscious even when he writes:

> Something had happen'd wrong about a bill
> That was not drawn with true mercantile skill;
> So to amend it I was told to go
> And seek the firm of Clutterbuck and Co.;

or again:

> We saw my Lord, and Lady Jane was there,
> And said to Johnson, 'Johnson, take a chair'.

Impossible, you may say—the bathos must be absolutely deliberate! The reader of Crabbe at large, however, and of those almost illiterate letters of his old age (so hard to reconcile with the fine letter to Burke), can never feel sure, as with Jane Austen we feel sure, that he knows what he is doing. At times it seems as if literary English were something of a foreign tongue to him; there are lapses in his grammar; so there are, for that matter, in Jane Austen's; but where she paints on her 'two inches of ivory', he works more crudely on a tile from the domestic hearth. There is, however, still another link between him and the authoress of *Northanger Abbey* in the fun both make of romantic extravaganzas and the goblin posterity of Horace Walpole and Mrs Radcliffe:

> banditti who, in forest wide
> And cavern vast, indignant virgins hide;
> Who, hemm'd with bands of sturdiest rogues about,
> Find some strange succour, and come virgins out.

(Which reads—so little do human appetites change—strangely like an account of a modern film melodrama.) Yet there is also a difference. Crabbe mocked romanticism of this sort, but he had also loved it in his time, and devoured it. He is a realist, like Jane Austen, but the realist of a wider, as well as lower, world; and a realist far less single-minded and content to take life as it is. He laughs at dreams; but he envies them.

> Go on, then, Son of Vision! Still pursue
> Thy airy dreams; the world is dreaming too.
> Ambition's lofty views, the pomp of state,
> The pride of wealth, the splendour of the great,
> Stripp'd of their mask, their cares and troubles known,
> Are visions far less happy than thy own.

The lesson of life, in tale after tale of his, is simply to forget romance and accept reality; one of his heroines will deliberately school herself out of an unwise passion:

> I sought my remedies for these;
> I suffer'd common things my mind to please,
> And common pleasures; seldom walk'd alone,
> Nor when the moon upon the waters shone;
> But then my candles lit, my window closed,
> My needle took, and with my neighbours prosed:
> And in one year—nay, ere the end of one—
> My labour ended, and my love was done.

How sensible, and successful; and yet what a sad success, though not without its dignity! But such success was not to be Crabbe's own. He could not always draw his own curtains so firmly against the moonshine's lure. At sixty he was to woo a girl. In consequence, his view of life, despite his stoicism and his humour, remains intensely sad.

> Ah, world unknown! How charming is thy view;
> Thy pleasures many, and each pleasure new!
> Ah, world experienc'd, what of thee is told?
> How few thy pleasures, and those few how old!

His landscape lies under a grey light, very different from the dappled sunshine in Miss Austen's morning-room. Perhaps women are less often pessimists—or passionate pessimists—than men. Madame Ackermanns are rare. Crabbe has his English faith in the ultimate goodness of God, as a sort of Universal Landlord, rather absentee, who can be trusted to behave like a decent Englishman when the final audit comes. But this life, meanwhile, is not gay to watch. It is not the high tragedies that are hardest to bear: they come seldom, and he does not write of those. It is the long littleness of the common lot, the silent suffering, the growing weakness and squalor of the body, the progress of prose in the soul. 'Il y a horriblement de mal sur la terre'—the sense of that pressed harder on Crabbe than on Voltaire; but it also wrung from him some of his most real poetry. Set this picture of pauper graves beside Gray's *Country Churchyard*; it need not shrink from the comparison:

> There lie the happy dead, from trouble free,
> And the glad parish pays the frugal fee.
> No more, O Death, thy victim starts to hear
> Churchwarden stern or kingly overseer;
> No more the farmer claims his humble bow;
> Thou art his lord, the best of tyrants thou.

But a closer and clearer parallel is, of course, with Gray's enemy, who encouraged Crabbe's beginnings, Samuel Johnson. Both men had the same uncanting sense of the world's real sorrows and the same impatience with the imaginary ones of hypochondriacs:

> Who with mock patience dire complaints endure
> Which real pain, and that alone, can cure.

xxviii

And how easily might lines like these come from *The Vanity of Human Wishes!*—

> The rich man built a house both large and high;
> He enter'd in, and set him down to sigh;

or:

> Of Hermit Quarll we read, in island rare,
> Far from mankind, and seeming far from care;
> Safe from all want, and sound in every limb;
> Yes! there was he, and there was care with him;

or this picture of unrepentant age (though here, perhaps, the actual source is Dryden's *All for Love*):

> Like a sad traveller who, at closing day,
> Finds he has wander'd widely from his way,
> Yet wanders on, nor will new paths explore,
> Till the night falls and he can walk no more.

But Crabbe, with the strain of romance in his nature, is also in time a generation nearer than Johnson to the Romantic Revival. He is less afraid of letting his imagination go. Like a plebeian cousin of Landor, he, too, stands at the meeting of two centuries, between reason and dream. Johnson would never have written *Sir Eustace Grey*, that opium-stimulated nightmare which, however inferior to *Kubla Khan*, is a strange work for this solid Anglican; even though in deference to good sense he puts it in the mouth of a haunted lunatic:[1]

> They forced me on, where ever dwell
>   Far-distant men in cities fair,
> Cities of whom no travellers tell,
>   Nor feet but mine were wanderers there.
>
> Their watchmen stare, and stand aghast,
>   As on we hurry through the dark;
> The watch-light blinks as we go past,
>   The watch-dog shrinks and fears to bark.

[1] Scott applied a quotation from it to himself when his mind was beginning to fail.

But even when Crabbe rides away over the hills of romance, his grim realism rides behind him; he takes the road, not towards Xanadu, but towards Wuthering Heights. He never travels so far; but tales like *Smugglers and Poachers* or *Peter Grimes*, with its description of the spectres that haunt the fisherman who has murdered his apprentices, show both sides of Crabbe. If his romanticism calls up the accusing phantoms, it is his minutest realism that paints the setting— the slimy channels in the salt-marsh, the blighted tree, the melancholy stakes with their sun-blistered tar, the tepid, muddy waters,

> Where the small eels that left the deeper way
> For the warm shore, within the shallows play;
> Where gaping muscles, left upon the mud,
> Slope their slow passage to the fallen flood.
> Here, dull and hopeless, he'd lie down and trace
> How sidelong crabs had scrawl'd their crooked race,
> Or sadly listen to the tuneless cry
> Of fishing gull or clanging golden-eye;
> What time the sea-birds to the marsh would come,
> And the loud bittern, from the bull-rush home,
> Gave from the salt ditch side the bellowing boom:
> He nursed the feelings these dull scenes produce,
> And loved to stop beside the opening sluice,
> Where the small stream, confined in narrow bound,
> Ran with a dull, unvaried, sadd'ning sound.

The last two lines might be a description of Crabbe's own verse; and certainly the 'muscles' are a little difficult to swallow; but then we are meant to see the scene, not to like it. Those who are amused by contrasts should turn to the picture of this same Dunwich coast in Swinburne's *By the North Sea*. Nothing could be more different; there, on the contrary, we are meant to admire rather than to see:

Miles and miles and miles of desolation!
　　Leagues on leagues on leagues without a change!
Sign or token of some eldest nation
　　Here would make the strange land not so strange.
Time-forgotten, yea since Time's creation,
　　Seem these borders where the sea-birds range.

Crabbe indulges in no such flourishes, he is down on his knees among the bugloss and sea-lavender; but his landscapes are, perhaps, the most permanent part of his work. Here, too, he stands between two ages: Pope would have thought him too mean, Johnson too minute and precise, while Wordsworth and Coleridge found him too unimaginative. And yet even his portraits of human character will perhaps be outlived by these still-lifes and landscapes—such as that favourite of Tennyson's (whose *Enoch Arden* was indebted to Crabbe's *Parting Hour*):

But now dejected, languid, listless, low,
He saw the wind upon the water blow,
And the cold stream curl'd onward as the gale
From the pine-hill blew harshly down the dale...
Far to the left he saw the huts of men
Half hid in mist that hung upon the fen.
Before him swallows, gathering for the sea,
Took their short flights and twitter'd on the lea;
And, near, the bean-sheaf stood, the harvest done,
And slowly blacken'd in the sickly sun.

Or again:

Cold grew the foggy morn, the day was brief,
Loose on the cherry hung the crimson leaf;
The dew dwelt ever on the herb; the woods
Roar'd with strong blasts, with mighty showers the floods;
All green was vanish'd, save of pine and yew,
That still display'd their melancholy hue;
Save the green holly with its berries red,
And the green moss that o'er the gravel spread.

Or, bleaker still:

> And void of stars the angry clouds look down
> On the cold earth, exchanging frown with frown.

Yet more desolate, perhaps, than all his wintry landscapes is that still-life from a workhouse death-bed:

> A yellow teapot, standing at his side,
> From its half-spout the cold black tea supplied.

It is ludicrous, and yet it is also grisly, that teapot; and its tea seems venomous.

Crabbe wrote far too much (*The Borough* alone contains ten thousand lines), and rewrote far too little; but he is in himself a typical representative—more typical than most of our poets—of that nation of shopkeepers which has yet produced the finest body of poetry in the world. The stiff Saxon clay, the saving spark of Franco-Norman wit, the moral grimness of Langland and the humorous insight of Chaucer—we may fancy we can trace that double ancestry in him, as in many another writer of our race. His thick-ankled style has none of the grace of the pure French artists he sometimes distantly recalls—such as Guy de Maupassant, or the creator of Madame Bovary, whose tragedy of thwarted romanticism would have at once appealed to Crabbe. Even Balzac is elegant beside this homespun Englishman. And yet Fitzgerald's beloved 'old Man' keeps still some of the grey power of the native countryside he fondly painted—the quiet murmur of its lowland rivers with their willows, like his couplets, two and two; the desolate appeal of its wind-warped pines and lonely-blooming furze; the silver light of sunset on its still estuaries. It changes little with the passing of the seasons and the years; it endures where beauties of a more artificial culture wither and vanish without a trace.

INEBRIETY

THE VICAR

THE vicar at the table's front presides,
Whose presence a monastic life derides;
The reverend wig, in sideway order placed,
The reverend band, by rubric stains disgraced,
The leering eye, in wayward circles roll'd,
Mark him the pastor of a jovial fold,
Whose various texts excite a loud applause,
Favouring the bottle, and the good old cause.
See! the dull smile which fearfully appears,
When gross indecency her front uprears;
The joy conceal'd, the fiercer burns within,
As masks afford the keenest gust to sin;
Imagination helps the reverend sire,
And spreads the sails of sub-divine desire;
But when the gay immoral joke goes round,
When shame and all her blushing train are drown'd,
Rather than hear his God blasphemed, he takes
The last loved glass, and then the board forsakes.
Not that religion prompts the sober thought,
But slavish custom has the practice taught;
Besides, this zealous son of warm devotion
Has a true Levite bias for promotion.
Vicars must with discretion go astray,
Whilst bishops may be damn'd the nearest way.

*   *   *

*   *   *

Lo, all in silence, all in order stand,
   And mighty folios first, a lordly band;
   Then quartos their well-order'd ranks maintain,
And light octavos fill a spacious plain:
See yonder, ranged in more frequented rows,
A humbler band of duodecimos;
While undistinguish'd trifles swell the scene,
The last new play and fritter'd magazine.

OLD BOOKS AND NEW

*   *   *

Ah! needless now this weight of massy chain;
Safe in themselves, the once-loved works remain;
No readers now invade their still retreat,
None try to steal them from their parent-seat;
Like ancient beauties, they may now discard
Chains, bolts, and locks, and lie without a guard.
   Our patient fathers trifling themes laid by,
And roll'd, o'er labour'd works, th' attentive eye:
Page after page, the much-enduring men
Explored the deeps and shallows of the pen;
Till, every former note and comment known,
They mark'd the spacious margin with their own
Minute corrections proved their studious care;
The little index, pointing, told us where;
And many an emendation show'd the age
Look'd far beyond the rubric title-page.

Our nicer palates lighter labours seek,
Cloy'd with a folio-*Number* once a week;
Bibles, with cuts and comments, thus go down:
E'en light Voltaire is *number'd* through the town:
Thus physic flies abroad, and thus the law,
From men of study, and from men of straw;
Abstracts, abridgments, please the fickle times,
Pamphlets and plays, and politics and rhymes.

*   *   *

THEOLOGIANS

*   *   *

Dull though impatient, peevish though devout,
With wit disgusting, and despised without;
Saints in design, in execution men,
Peace in their looks, and vengeance in their pen.

*   *   *

An Athanasian here, in deep repose,
Sleeps with the fiercest of his Arian foes;
Socinians here with Calvinists abide,
And thin partitions angry chiefs divide;
Here wily Jesuits simple Quakers meet,
And Bellarmine has rest at Luther's feet.
Great authors, for the church's glory fired,
Are for the church's peace, to rest retired;
And close beside, a mystic, maudlin race,
Lie 'Crumbs of Comfort for the Babes of Grace'.

*   *   *

*   *   *

Some have their favourite ills, and each disease
Is but a younger branch that kills from these;
One to the gout contracts all human pain;
He views it raging in the frantic brain;
Finds it in fevers all his efforts mar,
And sees it lurking in the cold catarrh:
Bilious by some, by others nervous seen,
Rage the fantastic demons of the spleen;
And every symptom of the strange disease
With every system of the sage agrees.

   Ye frigid tribe, on whom I wasted long
The tedious hours, and ne'er indulged in song;
Ye first seducers of my easy heart,
Who promised knowledge ye could not impart;
Ye dull deluders, truth's destructive foes;
Ye sons of fiction, clad in stupid prose;
Ye treacherous leaders, who, yourselves in doubt,
Light up false fires, and send us far about;—
Still may yon spider round your pages spin,
Subtile and slow, her emblematic gin!
Buried in dust and lost in silence, dwell,
Most potent, grave, and reverend friends—farewell!

*   *   *

4

*   *   *

Hence, ye profane! I feel a former dread,
A thousand visions float around my head:
Hark! hollow blasts through empty courts resound,
And shadowy forms with staring eyes stalk round;
See! moats and bridges, walls and castles rise,
Ghosts, fairies, demons, dance before our eyes:
Lo! magic verse inscribed on golden gate,
And bloody hand that beckons on to fate:—
'And who art thou, thou little page, unfold?
'Say, doth thy lord my Claribel withhold?
'Go tell him straight, Sir Knight, thou must resign
'The captive queen;—for Claribel is mine'.
Away he flies; and now for bloody deeds,
Black suits of armour, masks, and foaming steeds;
The giant falls; his recreant throat I seize,
And from his corslet take the massy keys:—
Dukes, lords, and knights in long procession move,
Released from bondage with my virgin love:—
She comes! she comes! in all the charms of youth,
Unequall'd love, and unsuspected truth!

Ah! happy he who thus, in magic themes,
O'er worlds bewitch'd, in early rapture dreams,
Where wild Enchantment waves her potent wand,
And Fancy's beauties fill her fairy land.

*   *   *

But lost, for ever lost, to me these joys,
Which Reason scatters, and which Time destroys;
Too dearly bought: maturer judgment calls
My busied mind from tales and madrigals;
My doughty giants all are slain or fled,
And all my knights—blue, green, and yellow—dead!
No more the midnight fairy tribe I view,
All in the merry moonshine tippling dew;
E'en the last lingering fiction of the brain,
The churchyard ghost, is now at rest again;
And all these wayward wanderings of my youth
Fly Reason's power, and shun the light of Truth.

*   *   *

CRITICS

*   *   *

Foes to our race! if ever ye have known
A father's fears for offspring of your own;
If ever, smiling o'er a lucky line,
Ye thought the sudden sentiment divine,
Then paused and doubted, and then, tired of doubt,
With rage as sudden dash'd the stanza out;—
If, after fearing much and pausing long,
Ye ventured on the world your labour'd song,
And from the crusty critics of those days
Implored the feeble tribute of their praise;
Remember now the fears that moved you then,
And, spite of truth, let mercy guide your pen.

*   *   *

*　　　*　　　*

'Happy for men in every age and clime,
'If all the sons of vision dealt in rhyme.
'Go on, then, Son of Vision! still pursue
'Thy airy dreams; the world is dreaming too.
'Ambition's lofty views, the pomp of state,
'The pride of wealth, the splendour of the great,
'Stripp'd of their mask, their cares and troubles known,
'Are visions far less happy than thy own:
'Go on! and, while the sons of care complain,
'Be wisely gay and innocently vain;
'While serious souls are by their fears undone,
'Blow sportive bladders in the beamy sun,
'And call them worlds! and bid the greatest show
'More radiant colours in their worlds below.'

*　　　*　　　*

THE VILLAGE

BOOK I

*　　　*　　　*

No shepherds now, in smooth alternate verse,
Their country's beauty or their nymphs' rehearse;
Yet still for these we frame the tender strain,
Still in our lays fond Corydons complain,
And shepherds' boys their amorous pains reveal,
The only pains, alas! they never feel.

*　　　*　　　*

Then shall I dare these real ills to hide
In tinsel trappings of poetic pride?
  No; cast by Fortune on a frowning coast,
Which neither groves nor happy valleys boast;
Where other cares than those the Muse relates,
And other shepherds dwell with other mates;
By such examples taught, I paint the Cot,
As Truth will paint it, and as Bards will not.

*　　　　*　　　　*

  Lo! where the heath, with withering brake grown o'er,
Lends the light turf that warms the neighbouring poor;
From thence a length of burning sand appears,
Where the thin harvest waves its wither'd ears;
Rank weeds, that every art and care defy,
Reign o'er the land, and rob the blighted rye:
There thistles stretch their prickly arms afar,
And to the ragged infant threaten war;
There poppies nodding, mock the hope of toil;
There the blue bugloss paints the sterile soil;
Hardy and high, above the slender sheaf,
The slimy mallow waves her silky leaf;
O'er the young shoot the charlock throws a shade,
And clasping tares cling round the sickly blade;
With mingled tints the rocky coasts abound,
And a sad splendour vainly shines around.

*　　　　*　　　　*

Go! if the peaceful cot your praises share,
Go look within, and ask if peace be there;
If peace be his—that drooping weary sire,
Or theirs, that offspring round their feeble fire;

8

Or hers, that matron pale, whose trembling hand
Turns on the wretched hearth th' expiring brand!
   Nor yet can Time itself obtain for these
Life's latest comforts, due respect and ease;
For yonder see that hoary swain, whose age
Can with no cares except its own engage;
Who, propt on that rude staff, looks up to see
The bare arms broken from the withering tree,
On which, a boy, he climb'd the loftiest bough,
Then his first joy, but his sad emblem now.

      *   *   *

For now he journeys to his grave in pain;
The rich disdain him; nay the poor disdain.

      *   *   *

THE POOR-HOUSE

      *   *   *

   Theirs is yon House that holds the parish poor,
Whose walls of mud scarce bear the broken door;
There, where the putrid vapours, flagging, play,
And the dull wheel hums doleful through the day;—
There children dwell who know no parents' care;
Parents, who know no children's love, dwell there!
Heart-broken matrons on their joyless bed,
Forsaken wives, and mothers never wed;
Dejected widows with unheeded tears,
And crippled age with more than childhood fears;
The lame, the blind, and, far the happiest they!
The moping idiot, and the madman gay.

      *   *   *

Say, ye, opprest by some fantastic woes,
Some jarring nerve that baffles your repose;
Who press the downy couch, while slaves advance
With timid eye to read the distant glance;
Who with sad prayers the weary doctor tease,
To name the nameless ever new disease;
Who with mock patience dire complaints endure,
Which real pain and that alone can cure;
How would ye bear in real pain to lie,
Despised, neglected, left alone to die?

*   *   *

ITS DOCTOR

*   *   *

But soon a loud and hasty summons calls,
Shakes the thin roof, and echoes round the walls;
Anon, a figure enters, quaintly neat,
All pride and business, bustle and conceit;
With looks unalter'd by these scenes of woe,
With speed that, entering, speaks his haste to go,
He bids the gazing throng around him fly,
And carries fate and physic in his eye:
A potent quack, long versed in human ills,
Who first insults the victim whom he kills;
Whose murd'rous hand a drowsy Bench protect,
And whose most tender mercy is neglect.

Paid by the parish for attendance here,
He wears contempt upon his sapient sneer;
In haste he seeks the bed where Misery lies,
Impatience mark'd in his averted eyes;
And, some habitual queries hurried o'er,
Without reply, he rushes on the door.

*   *   *

*   *   *

Up yonder hill, behold how sadly slow
The bier moves winding from the vale below:
There lie the happy dead, from trouble free,
And the glad parish pays the frugal fee:
No more, O Death! thy victim starts to hear
Churchwarden stern, or kingly overseer;
No more the farmer claims his humble bow,
Thou art his lord, the best of tyrants thou!

*   *   *

BOOK II

SUNDAY AFTER CHURCH

*   *   *

Then rural beaux their best attire put on,
To win their nymphs, as other nymphs are won:
While those long wed go plain, and by degrees,
Like other husbands, quit their care to please.
Some of the sermon talk, a sober crowd,
And loudly praise, if it were preach'd aloud;
Some on the labours of the week look round,
Feel their own worth, and think their toil renown'd;
While some, whose hopes to no renown extend,
Are only pleased to find their labours end.

*   *   *

*　　　*　　　*

Nor are the nymphs that breathe the rural air
So fair as Cynthia's, nor so chaste as fair:
These to the town afford each fresher face,
And the clown's trull receives the peer's embrace;
From whom, should chance again convey her down,
The peer's disease in turn attacks the clown.

*　　　*　　　*

THE JUSTICE

*　　　*　　　*

Lo! at his throne the silent nymph appears,
Frail by her shape, but modest in her tears;
And while she stands abash'd, with conscious eye,
Some favourite female of her judge glides by,
Who views with scornful glance the strumpet's fate,
And thanks the stars that made her keeper great:
Near her the swain, about to bear for life
One certain evil, doubts 'twixt war and wife;
But, while the faltering damsel takes her oath,
Consents to wed, and so secures them both.

*　　　*　　　*

RICH AND POOR

*　　　*　　　*

Who, a short time in varied fortune past,
Die, and are equal in the dust at last.

*　　　*　　　*

THE NEWSPAPER

*   *   *

No anxious virgin flies to 'fair Tweed-side';
No injured husband mourns his faithless bride;
No duel dooms the fiery youth to bleed;
But through the town transpires each vent'rous deed.
Should some fair frail-one drive her prancing pair
Where rival peers contend to please the fair;
When, with new force, she aids her conquering eyes,
And beauty decks, with all that beauty buys:
Quickly we learn whose heart her influence feels,
Whose acres melt before her glowing wheels.

To these a thousand idle themes succeed,
Deeds of all kinds, and comments to each deed.
Here stocks, the state-barometers, we view,
That rise or fall by causes known to few;
Promotion's ladder who goes up or down;
Who wed, or who seduced, amuse the town;
What new-born heir has made his father blest;
What heir exults, his father now at rest.

*   *   *

NEWSPAPER POETRY

*   *   *

Last in these ranks, and least, their art's disgrace,
Neglected stand the Muses' meanest race;
Scribblers who court contempt, whose verse the eye
Disdainful views, and glances swiftly by:
This Poet's Corner is the place they choose,
A fatal nursery for an infant Muse;

Unlike that Corner where true Poets lie,
These cannot live, and they shall never die;
Hapless the lad whose mind such dreams invade,
And win to verse the talents due to trade.

Curb then, O youth! these raptures as they rise,
Keep down the evil spirit and be wise;
Follow your calling, think the Muses foes,
Nor lean upon the pestle and compose.

* * *

THE PARISH REGISTER

PART I

BAPTISMS

THE COCK-FIGHT

* * *

HERE his poor bird th' inhuman Cocker brings,
Arms his hard heel and clips his golden wings;
With spicy food th' impatient spirit feeds,
And shouts and curses as the battle bleeds.
Struck through the brain, deprived of both his eyes,
The vanquish'd bird must combat till he dies;
Must faintly peck at his victorious foe,
And reel and stagger at each feeble blow:
When fallen, the savage grasps his dabbled plumes,
His blood-stain'd arms, for other deaths assumes;
And damns the craven-fowl, that lost his stake,
And only bled and perish'd for his sake.

* * *

*   *   *

Pride lives with all; strange names our rustics give
To helpless infants, that their own may live;
Pleased to be known, they 'll some attention claim,
And find some by-way to the house of fame.
  The straightest furrow lifts the ploughman's art,
The hat he gain'd has warmth for head and heart;
The bowl that beats the greater number down
Of tottering nine-pins, gives to fame the clown;
Or, foil'd in these, he opes his ample jaws,
And lets a frog leap down, to gain applause;
Or grins for hours, or tipples for a week,
Or challenges a well-pinch'd pig to squeak:
Some idle deed, some child's preposterous name,
Shall make him known, and give his folly fame.

  To name an infant meet our village sires,
Assembled all as such event requires;
Frequent and full, the rural sages sate,
And speakers many urged the long debate,—
Some harden'd knaves, who roved the country
       round,
Had left a babe within the parish-bound.—
First, of the fact they question'd—'Was it true?'
The child was brought—'What then remained
       to do?'
'Was 't dead or living?' This was fairly proved,—
'T was pinch'd, it roar'd, and every doubt removed.
Then by what name th' unwelcome guest to call
Was long a question, and it posed them all;

For he who lent it to a babe unknown,
Censorious men might take it for his own:
They look'd about, they gravely spoke to all,
And not one *Richard* answer'd to the call.
Next they inquired the day, when, passing by,
Th' unlucky peasant heard the stranger's cry:
This known,—how food and raiment they might
    give,
Was next debated—for the rogue would live;
At last, with all their words and work content,
Back to their homes the prudent vestry went,
And *Richard Monday* to the workhouse sent.

    There was he pinch'd and pitied, thump'd and fed,
And duly took his beatings and his bread;
Patient in all control, in all abuse,
He found contempt and kicking have their use:
Sad, silent, supple; bending to the blow,
A slave of slaves, the lowest of the low;
His pliant soul gave way to all things base,
He knew no shame, he dreaded no disgrace.
It seem'd, so well his passions he suppress'd,
No feeling stirr'd his ever-torpid breast;
Him might the meanest pauper bruise and cheat,
He was a footstool for the beggar's feet;
His were the legs that ran at all commands;
They used on all occasions Richard's hands:
His very soul was not his own; he stole
As others order'd, and without a dole;
In all disputes, on either part he lied,
And freely pledged his oath on either side;
In all rebellions Richard join'd the rest,
In all detections Richard first confess'd:

Yet, though disgraced, he watch'd his time so well,
He rose in favour, when in fame he fell;
Base was his usage, vile his whole employ,
And all despised and fed the pliant boy.
At length, ''T is time he should abroad be sent',
Was whisper'd near him,—and abroad he went;
One morn they call'd him, Richard answer'd not;
They deem'd him hanging, and in time forgot,—
Yet miss'd him long, as each throughout the clan
Found he 'had better spared a better man'.

Now Richard's talents for the world were fit,
He 'd no small cunning, and had some small wit;
Had that calm look which seem'd to all assent,
And that complacent speech which nothing meant:
He 'd but one care, and that he strove to hide—
How best for Richard Monday to provide.
Steel, through opposing plates, the magnet draws,
And steely atoms culls from dust and straws;
And thus our hero, to his interest true,
Gold through all bars and from each trifle drew;
But still more surely round the world to go,
This fortune's child had neither friend nor foe.

Long lost to us, at last our man we trace,—
'Sir Richard Monday died at Monday-place':
His lady's worth, his daughter's, we peruse,
And find his grandsons all as rich as Jews:
He gave reforming charities a sum,
And bought the blessings of the blind and dumb;
Bequeathed to missions money from the stocks,
And Bibles issued from his private box;
But to his native place severely just,
He left a pittance bound in rigid trust;—

Two paltry pounds, on every quarter's-day,
(At church produced) for forty loaves should pay;
A stinted gift, that to the parish shows
He kept in mind their bounty and their blows!

*   *   *

PART II

MARRIAGES

ENFORCED MARRIAGE

*   *   *

Next at our altar stood a luckless pair,
Brought by strong passions and a warrant there;
By long rent cloak, hung loosely, strove the bride,
From every eye, what all perceived, to hide.
While the boy-bridegroom, shuffling in his pace,
Now hid awhile and then exposed his face;
As shame alternately with anger strove
The brain confused with muddy ale to move,
In haste and stammering he perform'd his part,
And look'd the rage that rankled in his heart;
(So will each lover inly curse his fate,
Too soon made happy and made wise too late:)
I saw his features take a savage gloom,
And deeply threaten for the days to come.
Low spake the lass, and lisp'd and minced the while,
Look'd on the lad, and faintly tried to smile;
With soften'd speech and humbled tone she strove
To stir the embers of departed love:
While he, a tyrant, frowning walk'd before,
Felt the poor purse, and sought the public door,
She sadly following, in submission went,
And saw the final shilling foully spent;

18

Then to her father's hut the pair withdrew,
And bade to love and comfort long adieu!
  Ah! fly temptation, youth, refrain! refrain!
  I preach for ever; but I preach in vain!

*   *   *

RUSTIC CALLIGRAPHY

*   *   *

Behold these marks uncouth! how strange that men
Who guide the plough, should fail to guide the pen:
For half a mile the furrows even lie;
For half an inch the letters stand awry.

*   *   *

LUCY COLLINS

*   *   *

For *Lucy Collins* happier days had been,
Had Footman Daniel scorn'd his native green,
Or when he came an idle coxcomb down,
Had he his love reserved for lass in town;
To Stephen Hill she then had pledged her truth,—
A sturdy, sober, kind, unpolish'd youth;
But from the day, that fatal day she spied
The pride of Daniel, Daniel was her pride.
In all concerns was Stephen just and true;
But coarse his doublet was and patch'd in view,
And felt his stockings were, and blacker than his shoe;
While Daniel's linen all was fine and fair,—
His master wore it, and he deign'd to wear:
(To wear his livery, some respect might prove;
To wear his linen, must be sign of love:)

Blue was his coat, unsoil'd by spot or stain;
His hose were silk, his shoes of Spanish grain;
A silver knot his breadth of shoulder bore;
A diamond buckle blazed his breast before—
Diamond he swore it was! and show'd it as he swore,
Rings on his fingers shone; his milk-white hand
Could pick-tooth case and box for snuff command:
And thus, with clouded cane, a fop complete,
He stalk'd, the jest and glory of the street.
Join'd with these powers, he could so sweetly sing,
Talk with such toss, and saunter with such swing;
Laugh with such glee, and trifle with such art,
That Lucy's promise fail'd to shield her heart.

Stephen, meantime, to ease his amorous cares,
Fix'd his full mind upon his farm's affairs;
Two pigs, a cow, and wethers half a score,
Increased his stock, and still he look'd for more.
He, for his acres few, so duly paid,
That yet more acres to his lot were laid;
Till our chaste nymphs no longer felt disdain,
And prudent matrons praised the frugal swain;
Who thriving well, through many a fruitful year,
Now clothed himself anew, and acted overseer.

Just then poor Lucy, from her friend in town
Fled in pure fear, and came a beggar down;
Trembling, at Stephen's door she knock'd for bread,-
Was chidden first, next pitied, and then fed;
Then sat at Stephen's board, then shared in Stephen's
    bed:
All hope of marriage lost in her disgrace,
He mourns a flame revived, and she a love of lace.

*   *   *

20

*　　　　*　　　　*

'T is here, assembled, while in space apart
Their husbands, drinking, warm the opening heart,
Our neighbouring dames, on festal days, unite,
With tongues more fluent and with hearts as light;
Theirs is that art, which English wives alone
Profess—a boast and privilege their own;
An art it is where each at once attends
To all, and claims attention from her friends,
When they engage the tongue, the eye, the ear,
Reply when list'ning, and when speaking hear.

*　　　　*　　　　*

PART III

BURIALS

THE LADY OF THE HALL

*　　　　*　　　　*

Next died the LADY who yon Hall possess'd,
And here they brought her noble bones to rest.
In Town she dwelt;—forsaken stood the Hall:
Worms ate the floors, the tap'stry fled the wall:
No fire the kitchen's cheerless grate display'd;
No cheerful light the long-closed sash convey'd:
The crawling worm, that turns a summer fly,
Here spun his shroud and laid him up to die
The winter-death:—upon the bed of state,
The bat shrill shrieking woo'd his flickering mate;

21

To empty rooms the curious came no more;
From empty cellars turn'd the angry poor,
And surly beggars cursed the ever-bolted door.
To one small room the steward found his way,
Where tenants follow'd to complain and pay;
Yet no complaint before the Lady came,
The feeling servant spared the feeble dame;
Who saw her farms with his observing eyes,
And answer'd all requests with his replies:—
She came not down, her falling groves to view;
Why should she know, what one so faithful knew?
Why come, from many clamorous tongues to hear,
What one so just might whisper in her ear?
Her oaks or acres, why with care explore;
Why learn the wants, the sufferings of the poor;
When one so knowing all their worth could trace,
And one so piteous govern'd in her place?

Lo! now, what dismal Sons of Darkness come,
To bear this Daughter of Indulgence home;
Tragedians all, and well-arranged in black!
Who nature, feeling, force, expression lack;
Who cause no tear, but gloomily pass by,
And shake their sables in the wearied eye,
That turns disgusted from the pompous scene,
Proud without grandeur, with profusion, mean!
The tear for kindness past affection owes;
For worth deceased the sigh from reason flows;
E'en well-feign'd passions for our sorrows call,
And real tears for mimic miseries fall:
But this poor farce has neither truth nor art,
To please the fancy or to touch the heart.

*   *   *

*   *   *

  Her neat small room, adorn'd with maiden-taste,
A clipp'd French puppy, first of favourites, graced:
A parrot next, but dead and stuff'd with art;
(For Poll, when living, lost the Lady's heart,
And then his life; for he was heard to speak
Such frightful words as tinged his Lady's cheek:)
Unhappy bird! who had no power to prove,
Save by such speech, his gratitude and love.
A grey old cat his whiskers lick'd beside;
A type of sadness in the house of pride.
The polish'd surface of an India chest,
A glassy globe, in frame of ivory, press'd;
Where swam two finny creatures; one of gold,
Of silver one; both beauteous to behold:—
All these were form'd the guiding taste to suit;
The beast well-manner'd and the fishes mute.
A widow'd Aunt was there, compell'd by need
The nymph to flatter and her tribe to feed;
Who veiling well her scorn, endured the clog,
Mute as the fish and fawning as the dog.

*   *   *

THE SEXTON

*   *   *

His eightieth year he reach'd, still undecay'd,
And rectors five to one close vault convey'd:—

*   *   *

His masters lost, he 'd oft in turn deplore,
And kindly add,—'Heaven grant, I lose no more!'

Yet, while he spake, a sly and pleasant glance
Appear'd at variance with his complaisance:
For, as he told their fate and varying worth,
He archly look'd,—'I yet may bear thee forth'.

 *   *   *

Yes; he is gone: and WE are going all;
Like flowers we wither, and like leaves we fall;
Here, with an infant, joyful sponsors come,
Then bear the new-made Christian to its home:
A few short years and we behold him stand
To ask a blessing, with his bride in hand:
A few, still seeming shorter, and we hear
His widow weeping at her husband's bier:—
Thus, as the months succeed, shall infants take
Their names; thus parents shall the child forsake;
Thus brides again and bridegrooms blithe shall kneel,
By love or law compell'd their vows to seal,
Ere I again, or one like me, explore
These simple Annals of the VILLAGE POOR.

SIR EUSTACE GREY

THE MADMAN'S DREAM

 *   *   *

THEN those ill-favour'd Ones, whom none
But my unhappy eyes could view,
Led me, with wild emotion, on,
And, with resistless terror, drew.
Through lands we fled, o'er seas we flew,
And halted on a boundless plain;
Where nothing fed, nor breathed, nor grew,
But silence ruled the still domain.

Upon that boundless plain, below,
    The setting sun's last rays were shed,
And gave a mild and sober glow,
    Where all were still, asleep, or dead;
Vast ruins in the midst were spread,
    Pillars and pediments sublime,
Where the grey moss had form'd a bed,
    And clothèd the crumbling spoils of time.

There was I fix'd, I know not how,
    Condemn'd for untold years to stay:
Yet years were not;—one dreadful *Now*
    Endured no change of night or day;
The same mild evening's sleeping ray
    Shone softly solemn and serene,
And all that time I gazed away,
    The setting sun's sad rays were seen.

At length a moment's sleep stole on,—
    Again came my commission'd foes;
Again through sea and land we 're gone,
    No peace, no respite, no repose:
Above the dark broad sea we rose,
    We ran through bleak and frozen land;
I had no strength their strength t' oppose,
    An infant in a giant's hand.

*   *   *

Slowly that darkness pass'd away,
    When down upon the earth I fell,—
Some hurried sleep was mine by day;
    But, soon as toll'd the evening bell,

They forced me on, where ever dwell
  Far-distant men in cities fair,
Cities of whom no travellers tell,
  Nor feet but mine were wanderers there.

Their watchmen stare, and stand aghast,
  As on we hurry through the dark;
The watch-light blinks as we go past,
  The watch-dog shrinks and fears to bark;
The watch-tower's bell sounds shrill; and, hark!
  The free wind blows—we 've left the town—
A wide sepulchral ground I mark,
  And on a tombstone place me down.

What monuments of mighty dead!
  What tombs of various kind are found!
And stones erect their shadows shed
  On humble graves, with wickers bound,
Some risen fresh, above the ground,
  Some level with the native clay:
What sleeping millions wait the sound,
  'Arise, ye dead, and come away!'

*   *   *

Those fiends upon a shaking fen
  Fix'd me, in dark tempestuous night;
There never trod the foot of men,
  There flock'd the fowl in wint'ry flight;
There danced the moor's deceitful light
  Above the pool where sedges grow;
And when the morning-sun shone bright,
  It shone upon a field of snow.

They hung me on a bough so small,
    The rook could build her nest no higher;
They fix'd me on the trembling ball
    That crowns the steeple's quiv'ring spire;
They set me where the seas retire,
    But drown with their returning tide;
And made me flee the mountain's fire,
    When rolling from its burning side.

*   *   *

I 've furl'd in storms the flapping sail,
    By hanging from the topmost-head;
I 've served the vilest slaves in jail,
    And pick'd the dunghill's spoil for bread;
I 've made the badger's hole my bed;
    I' ve wander'd with a gipsy crew;
I 've dreaded all the guilty dread,
    And done what they would fear to do.

*   *   *

THE BOROUGH

LETTER I

SUMMER SEA

*   *   *

THEN the broad bosom of the ocean keeps
    An equal motion; swelling as it sleeps,
    Then slowly sinking; curling to the strand,
Faint, lazy waves o'ercreep the rigid sand,
Or tap the tarry boat with gentle blow,
And back return in silence, smooth and slow.

*   *   *

THE VICAR

*   *   *

To what famed college we our Vicar owe,
To what fair county, let historians show:
Few now remember when the mild young man,
Ruddy and fair, his Sunday-task began;
Few live to speak of that soft soothing look
He cast around, as he prepared his book;
It was a kind of supplicating smile,
But nothing hopeless of applause the while;
And when he finished, his corrected pride
Felt the desert, and yet the praise denied.
Thus he his race began, and to the end
His constant care was, no man to offend;
No haughty virtues stirr'd his peaceful mind;
Nor urged the Priest to leave the Flock behind;
He was his Master's Soldier, but not one
To lead an army of his Martyrs on:
Fear was his ruling passion; yet was Love,
Of timid kind, once known his heart to move;
It led his patient spirit where it paid
Its languid offerings to a listening Maid:
She, with her widow'd Mother, heard him speak,
And sought awhile to find what he would seek:
Smiling he came, he smiled when he withdrew,
And paid the same attention to the two;
Meeting and parting without joy or pain,
He seem'd to come that he might go again.

The wondering girl, no prude, but something nice,
At length was chill'd by his unmelting ice;

She found her tortoise held such sluggish pace,
That she must turn and meet him in the chase:
This not approving, she withdrew, till one
Came who appear'd with livelier hope to run;
Who sought a readier way the heart to move,
Than by faint dalliance of unfixing love.

      *   *   *

   Yet our good priest to Joseph's praise aspired,
As once rejecting what his heart desired;
'I am escaped', he said, when none pursued;
When none attack'd him, 'I am unsubdued';
'Oh pleasing pangs of love!' he sang again,
Cold to the joy, and stranger to the pain.
E'en in his age would he address the young,
'I too have felt these fires, and they are strong';
But from the time he left his favourite maid,
To ancient females his devoirs were paid:
And still they miss him after Morning-prayer;
Nor yet successor fills the Vicar's chair,
Where kindred spirits in his praise agree,
A happy few, as mild and cool as he;
The easy followers in the female train,
Led without love, and captives without chain.
   Ye Lilies male! think (as your tea you sip,
While the town small-talk flows from lip to lip;
Intrigues half-gather'd, conversation-scraps,
Kitchen cabals, and nursery-mishaps)
If the vast world may not some scene produce,
Some state where your small talents might have use;
Within seraglios you might harmless move,
'Mid ranks of beauty, and in haunts of love;

There from too daring man the treasures guard,
An easy duty, and its own reward;
Nature's soft substitutes, you there might save
From crime the tyrant, and from wrong the slave.

* * *

Fiddling and fishing were his arts: at times
He alter'd sermons, and he aim'd at rhymes;
And his fair friends, not yet intent on cards,
Oft he amused with riddles and charades.
Mild were his doctrines, and not one discourse
But gain'd in softness what it lost in force.

* * *

Though mild benevolence our Priest possess'd,
'T was but by wishes or by words express'd.
Circles in water, as they wider flow,
The less conspicuous in their progress grow,
And when at last they touch upon the shore,
Distinction ceases, and they 're view'd no more.
His love, like that last circle, all embraced,
But with effect that never could be traced.

* * *

In him his flock found nothing to condemn;
Him sectaries liked,—he never troubled them.
No trifles fail'd his yielding mind to please,
And all his passions sunk in early ease;
Nor one so old has left this world of sin,
More like the being that he enter'd in.

* * *

LETTER IX

THE INVALID YOUNG LADY

*   *   *

She who will tremble if her eye explore
'The smallest monstrous mouse that creeps on floor';
Whom the kind doctor charged, with shaking head,
At early hour to quit the beaux for bed;
She has, contemning fear, gone down the dance,
Till she perceived the rosy morn advance;
Then has she wonder'd, fainting o'er her tea,
Her drops and julep should so useless be:
Ah! sure her joys must ravish every sense,
Who buys a portion at such vast expense.

*   *   *

LETTER X

AMENITIES OF WHIST

*   *   *

And hark! at other tables discord reigns,
With feign'd contempt for losses and for gains;
Passions awhile are bridled; then they rage,
In waspish youth, and in resentful age;
With scraps of insult—'Sir, when next you play,
'Reflect whose money 't is you throw away.
'No one on earth can less such things regard,
'But when one's partner doesn't know a card—'
   'I scorn suspicion, ma'am, but while you stand
'Behind that lady, pray keep down your hand.'
   'Good heav'n, revoke! remember, if the set
'Be lost, in honour you should pay the debt.'

'There, there's your money; but, while I have life,
'I 'll never more sit down with man and wife;
'They snap and snarl indeed, but in the heat
'Of all their spleen, their understandings meet,
'They are Freemasons, and have many a sign,
'That we, poor devils! never can divine:
'May it be told, do ye divide th' amount,
'Or goes it all to family account?'

*   *   *

LETTER XI

THE BOROUGH ROMEO

*   *   *

James in an evil hour went forth to woo
Young *Juliet Hart*, and was her Romeo:
They 'd seen the play, and thought it vastly sweet
For two young lovers by the moon to meet;
The nymph was gentle, of her favours free,
E'en at a word—no Rosalind was she;
Nor, like that other Juliet, tried his truth
With—'Be thy purpose marriage, gentle youth?'
But him received, and heard his tender tale
When sang the lark, and when the nightingale:
So in few months the generous lass was seen
I' the way that all the Capulets had been.

Then first repentance seized the amorous man,
And—shame on love!—he reason'd and he ran;
The thoughtful Romeo trembled for his purse,
And the sad sounds 'for better and for worse'.

*   *   *

INHABITANTS OF THE ALMS-HOUSE

CLELIA

Her lively and pleasant Manners—Her Reading and Decision—Her Intercourse
with different Classes of Society—Her Kind of Character—The favoured
Lover—Her Management of him: his of her—After one Period, Clelia with an
Attorney: her Manner and Situation there—Another such Period, when her
Fortune still declines—Mistress of an Inn—A Widow—Another such Interval:
she becomes poor and infirm, but still vain and frivolous—The fallen Vanity—
Admitted into the House: meets Blaney.

We had a sprightly nymph—in every town
Are some such sprights, who wander up and down;
She had her useful arts, and could contrive,
In Time's despite, to stay at twenty-five;—
'Here will I rest; move on, thou lying year,
'This is mine age, and I will rest me here'.

Arch was her look, and she had pleasant ways
Your good opinion of her heart to raise;
Her speech was lively, and with ease express'd,
And well she judged the tempers she address'd:
If some soft stripling had her keenness felt,
She knew the way to make his anger melt;
Wit was allow'd her, though but few could bring
Direct example of a witty thing;
'T was that gay, pleasant, smart, engaging speech,
Her beaux admired, and just within their reach;
Not indiscreet, perhaps, but yet more free
Than prudish nymphs allow their wit to be.

Novels and plays, with poems old and new,
Were all the books our nymph attended to;
Yet from the press no treatise issued forth,
But she would speak precisely of its worth.

She with the London stage familiar grew,
And every actor's name and merit knew;
She told how this or that their part mistook,
And of the rival Romeos gave the look;
Of either house 't was hers the strength to see,
Then judge with candour—'Drury Lane for me'.
  What made this knowledge, what this skill complete,
A fortnight's visit in Whitechapel Street.
  Her place in life was rich and poor between,
With those a favourite, and with these a queen;
She could her parts assume, and condescend
To friends more humble while an humble friend;
And thus a welcome, lively guest could pass,
Threading her pleasant way from class to class.
  'Her reputation?'—That was like her wit,
And seem'd her manner and her state to fit;
Something there was—what, none presumed to say;
Clouds lightly passing on a smiling day,—
Whispers and hints which went from ear to ear,
And mix'd reports no judge on earth could clear.
  But of each sex a friendly number press'd
To joyous banquets this alluring guest:
There, if indulging mirth, and freed from awe,
If pleasing all, and pleased with all she saw,
Her speech were free, and such as freely dwelt
On the same feelings all around her felt;
Or if some fond presuming favourite tried
To come so near as once to be denied;
Yet not with brow so stern or speech so nice,
But that he ventured on denial twice:—
If these have been, and so has Scandal taught,
Yet Malice never found the proof she sought.

34

But then came one, the Lovelace of his day,
Rich, proud, and crafty, handsome, brave, and gay;
Yet loved he not those labour'd plans and arts,
But left the business to the ladies' hearts,
And when he found them in a proper train,
He thought all else superfluous and vain:
But in that training he was deeply taught,
And rarely fail'd of gaining all he sought;
He knew how far directly on to go,
How to recede and dally to and fro;
How to make all the passions his allies,
And, when he saw them in contention rise,
To watch the wrought-up heart, and conquer by
    surprise.
  Our heroine fear'd him not; it was her part,
To make sure conquest of such gentle heart—
Of one so mild and humble; for she saw
In Henry's eye a love chastised by awe.
Her thoughts of virtue were not all sublime,
Nor virtuous all her thoughts; 't was now her time
To bait each hook, in every way to please,
And the rich prize with dext'rous hand to seize.
She had no virgin-terrors; she could stray
In all love's maze, nor fear to lose her way;
Nay, could go near the precipice, nor dread
A failing caution or a giddy head;
She 'd fix her eyes upon the roaring flood,
And dance upon the brink where danger stood.
  'T was nature all, she judged, in one so young,
To drop the eye and falter in the tongue;
To be about to take, and then command
His daring wish, and only view the hand:

Yes! all was nature; it became a maid
Of gentle soul t' encourage love afraid;—
He, so unlike the confident and bold,
Would fly in mute despair to find her cold:
The young and tender germ requires the sun
To make it spread; it must be smiled upon.
Thus the kind virgin gentle means devised,
To gain a heart so fond, a hand so prized;
More gentle still she grew; to change her way,
Would cause confusion, danger, and delay:
Thus (an increase of gentleness her mode),
She took a plain, unvaried, certain road,
And every hour believed success was near,
Till there was nothing left to hope or fear.

It must be own'd that, in this strife of hearts,
Man has advantage—has superior arts:
The lover's aim is to the nymph unknown,
Nor is she always certain of her own;
Or has her fears, nor these can so disguise,
But he who searches, reads them in her eyes,
In the avenging frown, in the regretting sighs:
These are his signals, and he learns to steer
The straighter course whenever they appear.

————

'Pass we ten years, and what was Clelia's fate?'
At an attorney's board alert she sate,
Not legal mistress: he with other men
Once sought her hand, but other views were then;
And when he knew he might the bliss command,
He other blessing sought, without the hand;
For still he felt alive the lambent flame,
And offer'd her a home,—and home she came.

There, though her higher friendships lived no
        more,
She loved to speak of what she shared before—
'Of the dear Lucy, heiress of the hall,—
'Of good Sir Peter,—of their annual ball,
'And the fair countess!—Oh! she loved them all!'
The humbler clients of her friend would stare,
The knowing smile,—but neither caused her care;
She brought her spirits to her humble state,
And soothed with idle dreams her frowning fate.

————

'Ten summers pass'd, and how was Clelia then?'—
Alas! she suffer'd in this trying ten;
The pair had parted: who to him attend,
Must judge the nymph unfaithful to her friend;
But who on her would equal faith bestow,
Would think him rash,—and surely she must know.
    Then as a matron Clelia taught a school,
But nature gave not talents fit for rule:
Yet now, though marks of wasting years were seen,
Some touch of sorrow, some attack of spleen;
Still there was life, a spirit quick and gay,
And lively speech and elegant array.
    The Griffin's landlord these allured so far,
He made her mistress of his heart and bar;
He had no idle retrospective whim,
Till she was his, her deeds concern'd not him:
So far was well,—but Clelia thought not fit
(In all the Griffin needed) to submit:
Gaily to dress and in the bar preside,
Soothed the poor spirit of degraded pride;
But cooking, waiting, welcoming a crew

Of noisy guests, were arts she never knew:
Hence daily wars, with temporary truce,
His vulgar insult, and her keen abuse;
And as their spirits wasted in the strife,
Both took the Griffin's ready aid of life;
But she with greater prudence—Harry tried
More powerful aid, and in the trial died;
Yet drew down vengeance: in no distant time,
Th' insolvent Griffin struck his wings sublime;—
Forth from her palace walk'd th' ejected queen,
And show'd to frowning fate a look serene;
Gay spite of time, though poor, yet well attired,
Kind without love, and vain if not admired.

———————

Another term is past; ten other years
In various trials, troubles, views, and fears:
Of these some pass'd in small attempts at trade;
Houses she kept for widowers lately made;
For now she said, 'They'll miss th' endearing friend,
'And I'll be there the soften'd heart to bend':
And true a part was done as Clelia plann'd—
The heart was soften'd, but she miss'd the hand;
She wrote a novel, and Sir Denys said
The dedication was the best he read;
But Edgeworths, Smiths, and Radcliffes so engross'd
The public ear, that all her pains were lost.
To keep a toy-shop was attempt the last,
There too she fail'd, and schemes and hopes were past
    Now friendless, sick, and old, and wanting bread,
The first-born tears of fallen pride were shed—
True, bitter tears; and yet that wounded pride,
Among the poor, for poor distinctions sigh'd.

Though now her tales were to her audience fit;
Though loud her tones, and vulgar grown her wit,
Though now her dress—(but let me not explain
The piteous patchwork of the needy-vain,
The flirtish form to coarse materials lent,
And one poor robe through fifty fashions sent);
Though all within was sad, without was mean,—
Still 't was her wish, her comfort, to be seen:
She would to plays on lowest terms resort,
Where once her box was to the beaux a court;
And, strange delight! to that same house where she
Join'd in the dance, all gaiety and glee,
Now with the menials crowding to the wall,
She 'd see, not share, the pleasures of the ball,
And with degraded vanity unfold,
How she too triumph'd in the years of old.
To her poor friends 't is now her pride to tell,
On what a height she stood before she fell;
At church she points to one tall seat, and 'There
We sat,' she cries, 'when my papa was mayor'.
Not quite correct in what she now relates,
She alters persons, and she forges dates;
And, finding memory's weaker help decay'd,
She boldly calls invention to her aid.

    Touch'd by the pity he had felt before,
For her Sir Denys oped the Alms-house door:
'With all her faults', he said, 'the woman knew
'How to distinguish—had a manner too;
'And, as they say she is allied to some
'In decent station—let the creature come'.

*   *   *

LETTER XVI
THE PLAIN-DEALER

*   *   *

'I speak my mind, I love the truth,' quoth he;
Till 't was his fate that useful truth to find,
'T is sometimes prudent not to speak the mind.

*   *   *

LETTER XVIII
THE WORKHOUSE

*   *   *

There, in one house, throughout their lives to be,
The pauper-palace which they hate to see:
That giant-building, that high-bounding wall,
Those bare-worn walks, that lofty thund'ring hall,
That large loud clock, which tolls each dreaded hour,
Those gates and locks, and all those signs of power;
It is a prison, with a milder name,
Which few inhabit without dread or shame.

*   *   *

Nothing to bring them joy, to make them weep,—
The day itself is, like the night, asleep;
Or on the sameness if a break be made,
'T is by some pauper to his grave convey'd;
By smuggled news from neighb'ring village told,
News never true, or truth a twelvemonth old;
By some new inmate doom'd with them to dwell,
Or justice come to see that all goes well;
Or change of room, or hour of leave to crawl
On the black footway winding with the wall,
Till the stern bell forbids, or master's sterner call.

Here too the mother sees her children train'd,
Her voice excluded and her feelings pain'd.

＊　　　＊　　　＊

Here nature's outrage serves no cause to aid;
The ill is felt, but not the Spartan made.

＊　　　＊　　　＊

The grateful hunter, when his horse is old,
Wills not the useless favourite to be sold;
He knows his former worth, and gives him place
In some fair pasture, till he runs his race:
But has the labourer, has the seaman done
Less worthy service, though not dealt to one?
Shall we not then contribute to their ease,
In their old haunts, where ancient objects please?
That, till their sight shall fail them, they may trace
The well-known prospect and the long-loved face.

＊　　　＊　　　＊

THE FISHER'S HUT

＊　　　＊　　　＊

Lo! yonder shed; observe its garden-ground,
With the low paling, form'd of wreck, around:
There dwells a Fisher; if you view his boat,
With bed and barrel—'t is his house afloat;
Look at his house, where ropes, nets, blocks, abound,
Tar, pitch, and oakum—'t is his boat aground.

＊　　　＊　　　＊

There, fed by food they love, to rankest size,
Around the dwellings docks and wormwood rise;

Here the strong mallow strikes her slimy root,
Here the dull nightshade hangs her deadly fruit:
On hills of dust the henbane's faded green,
And pencil'd flower of sickly scent is seen.

*　　　*　　　*

LETTER XIX

THE POOR OF THE BOROUGH

THE PARISH-CLERK

The Parish-Clerk began his Duties with the late Vicar, a grave and auster
Man; one fully orthodox; a Detecter and Opposer of the Wiles of Satan—H
Opinion of his own Fortitude—The more frail offended by these Professions—
His good Advice gives further Provocation—They invent Stratagems t
overcome his Virtue—His Triumph—He is yet not invulnerable: is assaulte
by fear of Want, and Avarice—He gradually yields to the Seduction—H
reasons with himself, and is persuaded—He offends, but with Terror; repea
his Offence; grows familiar with Crime: is detected—His Sufferings and Deat

With our late Vicar, and his age the same,
His Clerk, hight *Jachin*, to his office came;
The like slow speech was his, the like tall slender frame:
But Jachin was the gravest man on ground,
And heard his master's jokes with look profound;
For worldly wealth this man of letters sigh'd,
And had a sprinkling of the spirit's pride:
But he was sober, chaste, devout, and just,
One whom his neighbours could believe and trust:
Of none suspected, neither man nor maid
By him were wrong'd, or were of him afraid.
　　There was indeed a frown, a trick of state
In Jachin;—formal was his air and gait:
But if he seem'd more solemn and less kind,
Than some light men to light affairs confined,

42

Still 't was allow'd that he should so behave
As in high seat, and be severely grave.

  This book-taught man, to man's first foe profess'd
Defiance stern, and hate that knew not rest;
He held that Satan, since the world began,
In every act, had strife with every man;
That never evil deed on earth was done,
But of the acting parties he was one;
The flattering guide to make ill prospects clear;
To smooth rough ways the constant pioneer;
The ever-tempting, soothing, softening power,
Ready to cheat, seduce, deceive, devour.

  'Me has the sly Seducer oft withstood,'
Said pious Jachin,—'but he gets no good;
'I pass the house where swings the tempting sign,
'And pointing, tell him, "Satan, that is thine":
'I pass the damsels pacing down the street,
'And look more grave and solemn when we meet;
'Nor doth it irk me to rebuke their smiles,
'Their wanton ambling and their watchful wiles:
'Nay, like the good John Bunyan, when I view
'Those forms, I'm angry at the ills they do;
'That I could pinch and spoil, in sin's despite,
'Beauties, which frail and evil thoughts excite.

  'At feasts and banquets seldom am I found,
'And (save at church) abhor a tuneful sound;
'To plays and shows I run not to and fro,
'And where my master goes, forbear to go.'

  No wonder Satan took the thing amiss,
To be opposed by such a man as this—
A man so grave, important, cautious, wise,
Who dared not trust his feeling or his eyes;

No wonder he should lurk and lie in wait,
Should fit his hooks and ponder on his bait;
Should on his movements keep a watchful eye;
For he pursued a fish who led the fry.

With his own peace our Clerk was not content;
He tried, good man! to make his friends repent.
'Nay, nay, my friends, from inns and taverns fly;
'You may suppress your thirst, but not supply:
'A foolish proverb says, "the devil 's at home";
'But he is there, and tempts in every room:
'Men feel, they know not why, such places please;
'His are the spells—they 're idleness and ease;
'Magic of fatal kind he throws around,
'Where care is banish'd, but the heart is bound.
'Think not of Beauty;—when a maid you meet,
'Turn from her view and step across the street;
'Dread all the sex: their looks create a charm,
'A smile should fright you and a word alarm:
'E'en I myself, with all my watchful care,
'Have for an instant felt the insidious snare;
'And caught my sinful eyes at the endang'ring stare;
'Till I was forced to smite my bounding breast
'With forceful blow, and bid the bold-one rest.

'Go not with crowds when they to pleasure run,
'But public joy in private safety shun:
'When bells, diverted from their true intent,
'Ring loud for some deluded mortal sent
'To hear or make long speech in parliament;
'What time the many, that unruly beast,
'Roars its rough joy and shares the final feast;
'Then heed my counsel, shut thine ears and eyes;
'A few will hear me—for the few are wise.'

Not Satan's friends, nor Satan's self could bear,
The cautious man who took of souls such care;
An interloper,—one who, out of place,
Had volunteer'd upon the side of grace:
There was his master ready once a week
To give advice; what further need he seek?
'Amen, so be it':—what had he to do
With more than this?—'t was insolent and new;
And some determined on a way to see
How frail he was, that so it might not be.

First they essay'd to tempt our saint to sin,
By points of doctrine argued at an inn;
Where he might warmly reason, deeply drink,
Then lose all power to argue and to think.

In vain they tried; he took the question up,
Clear'd every doubt, and barely touch'd the cup:
By many a text he proved his doctrine sound,
And look'd in triumph on the tempters round.

Next 't was their care an artful lass to find,
Who might consult him, as perplex'd in mind;
She they conceived might put her case with fears,
With tender tremblings and seducing tears;
She might such charms of various kind display,
That he would feel their force and melt away:
For why of nymphs such caution and such dread,
Unless he felt, and fear'd to be misled?

She came, she spake: he calmly heard her case,
And plainly told her 't was a want of grace;
Bade her 'such fancies and affections check,
'And wear a thicker muslin on her neck'.
Abased, his human foes the combat fled,
And the stern Clerk yet higher held his head.

They were indeed a weak, impatient set,
But their shrewd prompter had his engines yet;
Had various means to make a mortal trip,
Who shunn'd a flowing bowl and rosy lip;
And knew a thousand ways his heart to move,
Who flies from banquets and who laughs at love.

Thus far the playful Muse has lent her aid,
But now departs, of graver theme afraid;
Her may we seek in more appropriate time,—
There is no jesting with distress and crime.

Our worthy Clerk had now arrived at fame,
Such as but few in his degree might claim;
But he was poor, and wanted not the sense
That lowly rates the praise without the pence:
He saw the common herd with reverence treat
The weakest burgess whom they chanced to meet;
While few respected his exalted views,
And all beheld his doublet and his shoes:
None, when they met, would to his parts allow
(Save his poor boys) a hearing or a bow:
To this false judgment of the vulgar mind,
He was not fully, as a saint, resign'd;
He found it much his jealous soul affect,
To fear derision and to find neglect.

The year was bad, the christening-fees were small,
The weddings few, the parties paupers all:
Desire of gain with fear of want combined,
Raised sad commotion in his wounded mind;
Wealth was in all his thoughts, his views, his dreams,
And prompted base desires and baseless schemes.

Alas! how often erring mortals keep
The strongest watch against the foes who sleep;

46

While the more wakeful, bold, and artful foe
Is suffer'd guardless and unmark'd to go.

Once in a month the sacramental bread
Our Clerk with wine upon the table spread:
The custom this, that as the vicar reads,
He for our off'rings round the church proceeds:
Tall spacious seats the wealthier people hid,
And none had view of what his neighbour did:
Laid on the box and mingled when they fell,
Who should the worth of each oblation tell?
Now as poor Jachin took the usual round,
And saw the alms and heard the metal sound,
He had a thought—at first it was no more
Than—'these have cash and give it to the poor'.
A second thought from this to work began—
'And can they give it to a poorer man?'
Proceeding thus,—'My merit could they know;
'And knew my need, how freely they'd bestow;
'But though they know not, these remain the same,
'And are a strong, although a secret claim:
'To me, alas! the want and worth are known;
'Why then, in fact, 't is but to take my own'.

Thought after thought pour'd in, a tempting train:—
'Suppose it done,—who is it could complain?
'How could the poor? for they such trifles share,
'As add no comfort, as suppress no care;
'But many a pittance makes a worthy heap,—
'What says the law? that silence puts to sleep:—
'Nought then forbids, the danger could we shun,
'And sure the business may be safely done.

'But am I earnest?—earnest? No.—I say,
'If such my mind, that I could plan a way;

'Let me reflect;—I've not allow'd me time
'To purse the pieces, and if dropp'd they'd chime':
Fertile is evil in the soul of man,—
He paused,—said Jachin, 'They may drop on bran.
'Why then 't is safe and (all consider'd) just,
'The poor receive it,—'t is no breach of trust:
'The old and widows may their trifles miss,
'There must be evil in a good like this:
'But I'll be kind—the sick I'll visit twice,
'When now but once, and freely give advice.
'Yet let me think again':—Again he tried,
For stronger reasons on his passion's side,
And quickly these were found, yet slowly he com-
    plied.

The morning came: the common service done,
Shut every door,—the solemn rite begun,—
And, as the priest the sacred sayings read,
The clerk went forward, trembling as he tread:
O'er the tall pew he held the box, and heard
The offer'd piece, rejoicing as he fear'd:
Just by the pillar, as he cautious tripp'd,
And turn'd the aisle, he then a portion slipp'd
From the full store, and to the pocket sent,
But held a moment—and then down it went.

The priest read on, on walk'd the man afraid,
Till a gold offering in the plate was laid:
Trembling he took it, for a moment stopp'd,
Then down it fell, and sounded as it dropp'd;
Amazed he started, for th' affrighted man,
Lost and bewilder'd, thought not of the bran.
But all were silent, all on things intent
Of high concern, none ear to money lent;

So on he walk'd, more cautious than before,
And gain'd the purposed sum and one piece more.
  'Practice makes perfect': when the month came
          round,
He dropp'd the cash, nor listen'd for a sound:
But yet, when last of all th' assembled flock
He ate and drank,—it gave th' electric shock:
Oft was he forced his reasons to repeat,
Ere he could kneel in quiet at his seat;
But custom soothed him—ere a single year
All this was done without restraint or fear:
Cool and collected, easy and composed,
He was correct till all the service closed;
Then to his home, without a groan or sigh,
Gravely he went, and laid his treasure by.
Want will complain: some widows had express'd
A doubt if they were favour'd like the rest;
The rest described with like regret their dole,
And thus from parts they reason'd to the whole:
When all agreed some evil must be done,
Or rich men's hearts grew harder than a stone.
  Our easy vicar cut the matter short;
He would not listen to such vile report.
  All were not thus—there govern'd in that year
A stern stout churl, an angry overseer;
A tyrant fond of power, loud, lewd, and most severe:
Him the mild vicar, him the graver clerk,
Advised, reproved, but nothing would he mark,
Save the disgrace; 'and that, my friends,' said he,
'Will I avenge, whenever time may be'.
And now, alas! 't was time;—from man to man
Doubt and alarm and shrewd suspicions ran.

With angry spirit and with sly intent,
This parish-ruler to the altar went:
A private mark he fix'd on shillings three,
And but one mark could in the money see:
Besides, in peering round, he chanced to note
A sprinkling slight on Jachin's Sunday-coat:
All doubt was over:—when the flock were bless'd,
In wrath he rose, and thus his mind express'd:—
'Foul deeds are here!' and saying this, he took
The Clerk, whose conscience, in her cold-fit, shook:
His pocket then was emptied on the place;
All saw his guilt; all witness'd his disgrace:
He fell, he fainted, not a groan, a look,
Escaped the culprit; 't was a final stroke—
A death-wound never to be heal'd—a fall
That all had witness'd, and amazed were all.

As he recover'd, to his mind it came,
'I owe to Satan this disgrace and shame':
All the seduction now appear'd in view;
'Let me withdraw', he said, and he withdrew:
No one withheld him, all in union cried,
E'en the avenger,—'We are satisfied':
For what has death in any form to give,
Equal to that man's terrors, if he live?

He lived in freedom, but he hourly saw
How much more fatal justice is than law;
He saw another in his office reign,
And his mild master treat him with disdain:
He saw that all men shunn'd him, some reviled,
The harsh pass'd frowning, and the simple smiled;
The town maintain'd him, but with some reproof,
'And clerks and scholars proudly kept aloof'.

50

In each lone place, dejected and dismay'd,
Shrinking from view, his wasting form he laid;
Or to the restless sea and roaring wind
Gave the strong yearnings of a ruin'd mind:
On the broad beach, the silent summer-day,
Stretch'd on some wreck, he wore his life away;
Or where the river mingles with the sea,
Or on the mud-bank by the elder tree,
Or by the bounding marsh-dyke, there was he:
And when unable to forsake the town,
In the blind courts he sate desponding down—
Always alone; then feebly would he crawl
The church-way walk, and lean upon the wall:
Too ill for this, he lay beside the door,
Compell'd to hear the reasoning of the poor:
He look'd so pale, so weak, the pitying crowd
Their firm belief of his repentance vow'd;
They saw him then so ghastly and so thin,
That they exclaim'd, 'Is this the work of sin?'
    'Yes,' in his better moments, he replied,
'Of sinful avarice and the spirit's pride;—
'While yet untempted, I was safe and well;
'Temptation came; I reason'd, and I fell:
'To be man's guide and glory I design'd,
'A rare example for our sinful kind;
'But now my weakness and my guilt I see,
'And am a warning—man, be warn'd by me!'
    He said, and saw no more the human face;
To a lone loft he went, his dying place,
And, as the vicar of his state inquired,
Turn'd to the wall and silently expired!

*   *   *

I 've often marvell'd, when, by night, by day,
I 've mark'd the manners moving in my way,
And heard the language and beheld the lives
Of lass and lover, goddesses and wives,
That books, which promise much of life to give,
Should show so little how we truly live.

*   *   *

LETTER XXII

THE POOR OF THE BOROUGH

PETER GRIMES

The Father of Peter a Fisherman—Peter's early Conduct—His Grief for the
old Man—He takes an Apprentice—The Boy's Suffering and Fate—A second
Boy: how he died—Peter acquitted—A third Apprentice—A Voyage by Sea:
the Boy does not return—Evil Report on Peter: he is tried and threatened—
Lives alone—His Melancholy and incipient Madness—Is observed and visited
—He escapes and is taken: is lodged in a parish-house: Women attend and
watch him—He speaks in a Delirium: grows more collected—His Account of
his Feelings and visionary Terrors previous to his Death.

Old *Peter Grimes* made fishing his employ,
His wife he cabin'd with him and his boy,
And seem'd that life laborious to enjoy:
To town came quiet Peter with his fish,
And had of all a civil word and wish.
He left his trade upon the Sabbath-day,
And took young Peter in his hand to pray:
But soon the stubborn boy from care broke loose,
At first refused, then added his abuse:

His father's love he scorn'd, his power defied,
But being drunk, wept sorely when he died.

Yes! then he wept, and to his mind there came
Much of his conduct, and he felt the shame,—
How he had oft the good old man reviled,
And never paid the duty of a child.

*   *   *

On an inn-settle, in his maudlin grief,
This he revolved, and drank for his relief.

Now lived the youth in freedom, but debarr'd
From constant pleasure, and he thought it hard;
Hard that he could not every wish obey,
But must awhile relinquish ale and play;
Hard! that he could not to his cards attend,
But must acquire the money he would spend.

With greedy eye he look'd on all he saw,
He knew not justice, and he laugh'd at law;
On all he mark'd, he stretch'd his ready hand;
He fish'd by water and he filch'd by land:
Oft in the night has Peter dropp'd his oar,
Fled from his boat, and sought for prey on shore;
Oft up the hedge-row glided, on his back
Bearing the orchard's produce in a sack,
Or farm-yard load, tugg'd fiercely from the stack;
And as these wrongs to greater numbers rose,
The more he look'd on all men as his foes.

He built a mud-wall'd hovel, where he kept
His various wealth, and there he oft-times slept;
But no success could please his cruel soul,
He wish'd for one to trouble and control;

He wanted some obedient boy to stand
And bear the blow of his outrageous hand;
And hoped to find in some propitious hour
A feeling creature subject to his power.

Peter had heard there were in London then,—
Still have they being!—workhouse-clearing men,
Who, undisturb'd by feelings just or kind,
Would parish-boys to needy tradesmen bind:
They in their want a trifling sum would take,
And toiling slaves of piteous orphans make.

Such Peter sought, and when a lad was found,
The sum was dealt him, and the slave was bound.
Some few in town observed in Peter's trap
A boy, with jacket blue and woollen cap;
But none inquired how Peter used the rope,
Or what the bruise that made the stripling stoop;
None could the ridges on his back behold,
None sought him shiv'ring in the winter's cold;
None put the question,—'Peter, dost thou give
'The boy his food?—What, man! the lad must live:
'Consider, Peter, let the child have bread,
'He 'll serve thee better if he 's stroked and fed'.
None reason'd thus—and some, on hearing cries,
Said calmly, 'Grimes is at his exercise'.

Pinn'd, beaten, cold, pinch'd, threaten'd, and abused—
His efforts punish'd and his food refused,—
Awake tormented,—soon aroused from sleep,—
Struck if he wept, and yet compell'd to weep,
The trembling boy dropp'd down and strove to pray,
Received a blow, and trembling turn'd away,

Or sobb'd and hid his piteous face;—while he,
The savage master, grinn'd in horrid glee:
He'd now the power he ever loved to show,
A feeling being subject to his blow.

Thus lived the lad, in hunger, peril, pain,
His tears despised, his supplications vain:
Compell'd by fear to lie, by need to steal,
His bed uneasy and unbless'd his meal,
For three sad years the boy his tortures bore,
And then his pains and trials were no more.

'How died he, Peter?' when the people said,
He growl'd—'I found him lifeless in his bed';
Then tried for softer tone, and sigh'd, 'Poor Sam
    is dead'.
Yet murmurs were there, and some questions ask'd—
How he was fed, how punish'd, and how task'd?
Much they suspected, but they little proved,
And Peter pass'd untroubled and unmoved.

Another boy with equal ease was found,
The money granted, and the victim bound;
And what his fate?—One night it chanced he fell
From the boat's mast and perish'd in her well,
Where fish were living kept, and where the boy
(So reason'd men) could not himself destroy:—

'Yes! so it was', said Peter, 'in his play,
'(For he was idle both by night and day),
'He climb'd the main-mast and then fell below';—
Then show'd his corpse, and pointed to the blow.
'What said the jury?'—they were long in doubt,
But sturdy Peter faced the matter out:

So they dismissed him, saying at the time,
'Keep fast your hatchway when you 've boys who
    climb'.
This hit the conscience, and he colour'd more
Than for the closest questions put before.

Thus all his fears the verdict set aside,
And at the slave-shop Peter still applied.

Then came a boy, of manners soft and mild,—
Our seamen's wives with grief beheld the child;
All thought (the poor themselves) that he was one
Of gentle blood, some noble sinner's son,
Who had, belike, deceived some humble maid,
Whom he had first seduced and then betray'd:—
However this, he seem'd a gracious lad,
In grief submissive, and with patience sad.

Passive he labour'd, till his slender frame
Bent with his loads, and he at length was lame:
Strange that a frame so weak could bear so long
The grossest insult and the foulest wrong;
But there were causes—in the town they gave
Fire, food, and comfort, to the gentle slave;
And though stern Peter, with a cruel hand,
And knotted rope, enforced the rude command,
Yet he consider'd what he 'd lately felt,
And his vile blows with selfish pity dealt.

One day such draughts the cruel fisher made,
He could not vend them in his borough-trade,
But sail'd for London-mart: the boy was ill,
But ever humbled to his master's will;

And on the river, where they smoothly sail'd,
He strove with terror and awhile prevail'd;
But new to danger on the angry sea,
He clung affrighten'd to his master's knee:
The boat grew leaky and the wind was strong,
Rough was the passage and the time was long;
His liquor fail'd, and Peter's wrath arose,—
No more is known—the rest we must suppose,
Or learn of Peter:—Peter says, he 'spied
'The stripling's danger and for harbour tried;
'Meantime the fish, and then th' apprentice died'.

The pitying women raised a clamour round,
And weeping said, 'Thou hast thy 'prentice drown'd'.

Now the stern man was summon'd to the hall,
To tell his tale before the burghers all:
He gave th' account; profess'd the lad he loved,
And kept his brazen features all unmoved.

The mayor himself with tone severe replied,—
'Henceforth with thee shall never boy abide;
'Hire thee a freeman, whom thou durst not beat,
'But who, in thy despite, will sleep and eat:
'Free thou art now!—again shouldst thou appear,
'Thou 'lt find thy sentence, like thy soul, severe'.

Alas! for Peter not a helping hand,
So was he hated, could he now command;
Alone he row'd his boat, alone he cast
His nets beside, or made his anchor fast:
To hold a rope or hear a curse was none,—
He toil'd and rail'd; he groan'd and swore alone.

Thus by himself compell'd to live each day,
To wait for certain hours the tide's delay;
At the same time the same dull views to see,
The bounding marsh-bank and the blighted tree;
The water only, when the tides were high,
When low, the mud half cover'd and half-dry;
The sun-burnt tar that blisters on the planks,
And bank-side stakes in their uneven ranks;
Heaps of entangled weeds that slowly float,
As the tide rolls by the impeded boat.

When tides were neap, and, in the sultry day,
Through the tall bounding mud-banks made their
    way,
Which on each side rose swelling, and below
The dark warm flood ran silently and slow;
There anchoring, Peter chose from man to hide,
There hang his head, and view the lazy tide
In its hot slimy channel slowly glide;
Where the small eels that left the deeper way
For the warm shore, within the shallows play;
Where gaping muscles, left upon the mud,
Slope their slow passage to the fallen flood;—
Here dull and hopeless he 'd lie down and trace
How sidelong crabs had scrawl'd their crooked race,
Or sadly listen to the tuneless cry
Of fishing gull or clanging golden-eye;
What time the sea-birds to the marsh would come,
And the loud bittern, from the bull-rush home,
Gave from the salt ditch side the bellowing boom:
He nursed the feelings these dull scenes produce,
And loved to stop beside the opening sluice;

Where the small stream, confined in narrow bound,
Ran with a dull, unvaried, sadd'ning sound;
Where all, presented to the eye or ear,
Oppress'd the soul with misery, grief, and fear.

Besides these objects, there were places three,
Which Peter seem'd with certain dread to see;
When he drew near them he would turn from each,
And loudly whistle till he pass'd the reach.

A change of scene to him brought no relief,
In town, 't was plain, men took him for a thief:
The sailors' wives would stop him in the street,
And say, 'Now, Peter, thou 'st no boy to beat':
Infants at play when they perceived him, ran,
Warning each other—'That's the wicked man':
He growl'd an oath, and in an angry tone
Cursed the whole place and wish'd to be alone.

Alone he was, the same dull scenes in view,
And still more gloomy in his sight they grew:
Though man he hated, yet employ'd alone
At bootless labour, he would swear and groan,
Cursing the shoals that glided by the spot,
And gulls that caught them when his arts could not.

Cold nervous tremblings shook his sturdy frame,
And strange disease—he couldn't say the name;
Wild were his dreams, and oft he rose in fright,
Waked by his view of horrors in the night,—
Horrors that would the sternest minds amaze,
Horrors that demons might be proud to raise:
And though he felt forsaken, grieved at heart,
To think he lived from all mankind apart;
Yet, if a man approach'd, in terrors he would start,

A winter pass'd since Peter saw the town,
And summer lodgers were again come down;
These, idly curious, with their glasses spied
The ships in bay as anchor'd for the tide,—
The river's craft,—the bustle of the quay,—
And sea-port views, which landmen love to see.

One, up the river, had a man and boat
Seen day by day, now anchor'd, now afloat;
Fisher he seem'd, yet used no net nor hook;
Of sea-fowl swimming by no heed he took,
But on the gliding waves still fix'd his lazy look:
At certain stations he would view the stream,
As if he stood bewilder'd in a dream,
Or that some power had chain'd him for a time,
To feel a curse or meditate on crime.

This known, some curious, some in pity went,
And others question'd—'Wretch, dost thou repent?'
He heard, he trembled, and in fear resign'd
His boat: new terror fill'd his restless mind;
Furious he grew, and up the country ran,
And there they seized him—a distemper'd man:—
Him we received, and to a parish-bed,
Follow'd and cursed, the groaning man was led.

Here when they saw him, whom they used to shun,
A lost, lone man, so harass'd and undone;
Our gentle females, ever prompt to feel,
Perceived compassion on their anger steal;
His crimes they could not from their memories blot,
But they were grieved, and trembled at his lot.

A Priest too came, to whom his words are told;
And all the signs they shudder'd to behold.

'Look! look!' they cried; 'his limbs with horror shake,
'And as he grinds his teeth, what noise they make!
'How glare his angry eyes, and yet he's not awake:
'See! what cold drops upon his forehead stand,
'And how he clenches that broad bony hand.'

The Priest attending, found he spoke at times
As one alluding to his fears and crimes;
'It was the fall,' he mutter'd, 'I can show
'The manner how,—I never struck a blow':—
And then aloud,—'Unhand me, free my chain;
'On oath he fell—it struck him to the brain:—
'Why ask my father?—that old man will swear
'Against my life; besides, he wasn't there:
'What, all agreed?—Am I to die to-day?—
'My Lord, in mercy give me time to pray'.

Then as they watch'd him, calmer he became,
And grew so weak he couldn't move his frame,
But murmuring spake—while they could see and hear
The start of terror and the groan of fear;
See the large dew-beads on his forehead rise,
And the cold death-drop glaze his sunken eyes:
Nor yet he died, but with unwonted force
Seem'd with some fancied being to discourse:
He knew not us, or with accustom'd art
He hid the knowledge, yet exposed his heart;
'T was part confession and the rest defence,
A madman's tale, with gleams of waking sense.

'I'll tell you all,' he said, 'the very day
'When the old man first placed them in my way:
'My father's spirit—he who always tried
'To give me trouble, when he lived and died—

'When he was gone he could not be content
'To see my days in painful labour spent,
'But would appoint his meetings, and he made
'Me watch at these, and so neglect my trade.

''T was one hot noon, all silent, still, serene,
'No living being had I lately seen;
'I paddled up and down and dipp'd my net,
'But (such his pleasure) I could nothing get,—
'A father's pleasure, when his toil was done,
'To plague and torture thus an only son!
'And so I sat and look'd upon the stream,
'How it ran on, and felt as in a dream:
'But dream it was not: No!—I fix'd my eyes
'On the mid stream and saw the spirits rise:
'I saw my father on the water stand,
'And hold a thin pale boy in either hand;
'And there they glided ghastly on the top
'Of the salt flood, and never touch'd a drop:
'I would have struck them, but they knew th'
       intent,
'And smiled upon the oar, and down they went.

'Now, from that day, whenever I began
'To dip my net, there stood the hard old man—
'He and those boys: I humbled me and pray'd
'They would be gone; they heeded not, but stay'd:
'Nor could I turn, nor would the boat go by,
'But, gazing on the spirits, there was I:
'They bade me leap to death, but I was loth to die:
'And every day, as sure as day arose,
'Would these three spirits meet me ere the close;

'To hear and mark them daily was my doom,
'And "Come", they said, with weak, sad voices,
        "come".
'To row away, with all my strength I tried,
'But there were they, hard by me in the tide,
'The three unbodied forms—and "Come", still
        "come", they cried.

    'Fathers should pity—but this old man shook
'His hoary locks, and froze me by a look:
'Thrice, when I struck them, through the water came
'A hollow groan, that weaken'd all my frame:
'"Father!" said I, "have mercy":—he replied,
'I know not what—the angry spirit lied,—
'"Didst thou not draw thy knife?" said he:—
        'T was true,
'But I had pity and my arm withdrew:
'He cried for mercy, which I kindly gave,
'But he has no compassion in his grave.

    'There were three places, where they ever rose,—
'The whole long river has not such as those—
'Places accursed, where, if a man remain,
'He 'll see the things which strike him to the brain;
'And there they made me on my paddle lean,
'And look at them for hours;—accursed scene!
'When they would glide to that smooth eddy-space,
'Then bid me leap and join them in the place;
'And at my groans each little villain sprite
'Enjoy'd my pains and vanish'd in delight.

    'In one fierce summer-day, when my poor brain
'Was burning hot, and cruel was my pain,

'Then came this father-foe, and there he stood
'With his two boys again upon the flood:
'There was more mischief in their eyes, more glee
'In their pale faces, when they glared at me:
'Still did they force me on the oar to rest,
'And when they saw me fainting and oppress'd,
'He with his hand, the old man, scoop'd the flood,
'And there came flame about him mix'd with blood;
'He bade me stoop and look upon the place,
'Then flung the hot-red liquor in my face;
'Burning it blazed, and then I roar'd for pain,
'I thought the demons would have turn'd my brain.

'Still there they stood, and forced me to behold
'A place of horrors—they can not be told—
'Where the flood open'd, there I heard the shriek
'Of tortured guilt—no earthly tongue can speak:
'"All days alike! for ever!" did they say,
'"And unremitted torments every day"—
'Yes, so they said'—But here he ceased, and gazed
On all around, affrighten'd and amazed;
And still he tried to speak, and look'd in dread
Of frighten'd females gathering round his bed;
Then dropp'd exhausted, and appear'd at rest,
Till the strong foe the vital powers possess'd;
Then with an inward, broken voice he cried,
'Again they come!' and mutter'd as he died.

LETTER XXIII

THE HIGHWAYMAN'S DREAM BEFORE EXECUTION

* * *

Then through the broomy bound with ease they pass,
And press the sandy sheep-walk's slender grass,
Where dwarfish flowers among the gorse are spread,
And the lamb browses by the linnet's bed;
Then 'cross the bounding brook they make their way
O'er its rough bridge—and there behold the bay!—
The ocean smiling to the fervid sun—
The waves that faintly fall and slowly run—
The ships at distance and the boats at hand;
And now they walk upon the sea-side sand,
Counting the number and what kind they be,
Ships softly sinking in the sleepy sea.

* * *

LETTER XXIV

THE COLLEGE FELLOW

* * *

But fix our Scholar, and suppose him crown'd
With all the glory gain'd on classic ground;
Suppose the world without a sigh resign'd,
And to his college all his care confined;
Give him all honours that such states allow,
The freshman's terror and the tradesman's bow;
Let his apartments with his taste agree,
And all his views be those he loves to see;
Let him each day behold the savoury treat,
For which he pays not, but is paid to eat;

These joys and glories soon delight no more,
Although withheld, the mind is vex'd and sore;
The honour too is to the place confined,
Abroad they know not each superior mind:
Strangers no *wranglers* in these figures see,
Nor give they worship to a high degree;
Unlike the prophet's is the scholar's case,
His honour all is in his dwelling-place:
And there such honours are familiar things;
What is a monarch in a crowd of kings?
Like other sovereigns he 's by forms address'd,
By statutes govern'd and with rules oppress'd.

When all these forms and duties die away,
And the day passes like the former day,
Then of exterior things at once bereft,
He 's to himself and one attendant left;
Nay, John too goes[1]; nor aught of service more
Remains for him; he gladly quits the door,
And, as he whistles to the college-gate,
He kindly pities his poor master's fate.

* * *

INFANCY—A FRAGMENT

* * *

Joys are like oil; if thrown upon the tide
Of flowing life, they mix not, nor subside:
Griefs are like waters on the river thrown,
They mix entirely, and become its own.

* * *

[1] The sensation of loneliness felt by a fellow of a college when his servant left him for the night, was very feelingly described to Mr Crabbe by the late Mr Lambert, one of the senior fellows of Trinity College, Cambridge, and made a strong impression on the poet's mind. (Note by Crabbe's son.)

ON RECEIVING FROM A LADY
A PRESENT OF A RING

*   *   *

AND what shall I return the fair
    And flattering nymph?—A verse?—
      a prayer?
For were a Ring my present too,
I see the smile that must ensue;—
The smile that pleases though it stings,
And says—'No more of giving rings:
Remember, thirty years are gone,
Old friend! since you presented one!'

*   *   *

TALES

TALE II

THE PARTING HOUR

YOUNG LOVE

*   *   *

THUS early prudent and sedate they grew,
    While lovers, thoughtful—and though
      children, true.
To either parents not a day appear'd,
When with this love they might have interfered.
Childish at first, they cared not to restrain;
And strong at last, they saw restriction vain;
Nor knew they when that passion to reprove,
Now idle fondness, now resistless love.

*   *   *

THE GENTLEMAN FARMER

* * *

He was of those whose skill assigns the prize
For creatures fed in pens, and stalls, and sties;
And who, in places where improvers meet,
To fill the land with fatness, had a seat;
Who in large mansions live like petty kings,
And speak of farms but as amusing things;
Who plans encourage, and who journals keep,
And talk with lords about a breed of sheep.

* * *

Wisdom like this, as all things rich and rare,
Must be acquired with pains, and kept with care;
In books he sought it, which his friends might view,
When their kind host the guarding curtain drew.
There were historic works for graver hours,
And lighter verse to spur the languid powers;
There metaphysics, logic there had place;
But of devotion not a single trace—
Save what is taught in Gibbon's florid page,
And other guides of this inquiring age.
There Hume appear'd, and near a splendid book
Composed by Gay's 'good lord of Bolingbroke':
With these were mix'd the light, the free, the vain,
And from a corner peep'd the sage Tom Paine:
Here four neat volumes Chesterfield were named,
For manners much and easy morals famed;
With chaste Memoirs of females, to be read
When deeper studies had confused the head.

Such his resources, treasures where he sought
For daily knowledge till his mind was fraught:
Then, when his friends were present, for their use
He would the riches he had stored produce;
He found his lamp burn clearer when each day
He drew for all he purposed to display;
For these occasions, forth his knowledge sprung,
As mustard quickens on a bed of dung:
All was prepared, and guests allow'd the praise
For what they saw he could so quickly raise.

Such this new friend; and when the year came
      round,
The same impressive, reasoning sage was found:
Then, too, was seen the pleasant mansion graced
With a fair damsel—his no vulgar taste;
The neat *Rebecca*—sly, observant, still,
Watching his eye, and waiting on his will;
Simple yet smart her dress, her manners meek,
Her smiles spoke for her, she would seldom speak:
But watch'd each look, each meaning to detect,
And (pleased with notice) felt for all neglect.

With her lived Gwyn a sweet harmonious life,
Who, forms excepted, was a charming wife:
The wives indeed, so made by vulgar law,
Affected scorn, and censured what they saw,
And what they saw not, fancied; said 't was sin,
And took no notice of the wife of Gwyn:
But he despised their rudeness, and would prove
Theirs was compulsion and distrust, not love;
'Fools as they were! could they conceive that rings
'And parsons' blessings were substantial things?'

They answer'd 'Yes'; while he contemptuous spoke
Of the low notions held by simple folk;
Yet, strange that anger in a man so wise
Should from the notions of these fools arise;
Can they so vex us, whom we so despise?

Brave as he was, our hero felt a dread
Lest those who saw him kind should think him led;
If to his bosom fear a visit paid,
It was, lest he should be supposed afraid:
Hence sprang his orders; not that he desired
The things when done: obedience he required;
And thus, to prove his absolute command,
Ruled every heart, and moved each subject hand;
Assent he ask'd for every word and whim,
To prove that *he alone was king of him.*

*   *   *

TALE V

THE PATRON

GOLDSMITH

*   *   *

Genius is jealous: I have heard of some
Who, if, unnoticed, grew perversely dumb;
Nay, different talents would their envy raise;
Poets have sicken'd at a dancer's praise;
And one, the happiest writer of his time,
Grew pale at hearing Reynolds was sublime;
That Rutland's Duchess wore a heavenly smile—
'And I', said he, 'neglected all the while!'

*   *   *

*　　　*　　　*

'When ladies sing, or in thy presence play,
'Do not, dear John, in rapture melt away;
''T is not thy part, there will be list'ners round,
'To cry *Divine!* and dote upon the sound;
'Remember, too, that though the poor have ears,
'They take not in the music of the spheres;
'They must not feel the warble and the thrill,
'Or be dissolved in ecstasy at will;
'Beside, 't is freedom in a youth like thee
'To drop his awe, and deal in ecstasy!'

*　　　*　　　*

'Of all be cautious—but be most afraid
'Of the pale charms that grace My Lady's Maid;
'Of those sweet dimples, of that fraudful eye,
'The frequent glance designed for thee to spy;
'The soft bewitching look, the fond bewailing sigh:
'Let others frown and envy; she the while
'(Insidious syren!) will demurely smile;
'And for her gentle purpose, every day
'Inquire thy wants, and meet thee in thy way;
'She has her blandishments, and, though so weak,
'Her person pleases, and her actions speak:
'At first her folly may her aim defeat;
'But kindness shown, at length will kindness meet:
'Have some offended? them will she disdain,
'And, for thy sake, contempt and pity feign;
'She hates the vulgar, she admires to look
'On woods and groves, and dotes upon a book;

'Let her once see thee on her features dwell,
'And hear one sigh, then liberty farewell.

'But, John, remember we cannot maintain
'A poor, proud girl, extravagant and vain.'

*   *   *

TALE VI

THE FRANK COURTSHIP

Grave *Jonas Kindred*, Sybil Kindred's sire,
Was six feet high, and look'd six inches higher;
Erect, morose, determined, solemn, slow,
Who knew the man could never cease to know:
His faithful spouse, when Jonas was not by,
Had a firm presence and a steady eye;
But with her husband dropp'd her look and tone,
And Jonas ruled unquestion'd and alone.

He read, and oft would quote the sacred words,
How pious husbands of their wives were lords;
Sarah called Abraham Lord! and who could be,
So Jonas thought, a greater man than he?
Himself he view'd with undisguised respect,
And never pardon'd freedom or neglect.

They had one daughter, and this favourite child
Had oft the father of his spleen beguiled;
Soothed by attention from her early years,
She gained all wishes by her smiles or tears:
But *Sybil* then was in that playful time,
When contradiction is not held a crime;
When parents yield their children idle praise
For faults corrected in their after days.

Peace in the sober house of Jonas dwelt,
Where each his duty and his station felt:
Yet not that peace some favour'd mortals find,
In equal views and harmony of mind;
Not the soft peace that blesses those who love,
Where all with one consent in union move;
But it was that which one superior will
Commands, by making all inferiors still;
Who bids all murmurs, all objections cease,
And with imperious voice announces—Peace!

They were, to wit, a remnant of that crew,
Who, as their foes maintain, their Sovereign slew;
An independent race, precise, correct,
Who ever married in the kindred sect:
No son or daughter of their order wed
A friend to England's king who lost his head;
Cromwell was still their Saint, and when they met,
They mourn'd that Saints were not our rulers yet.

Fix'd were their habits; they arose betimes,
Then pray'd their hour, and sang their party-rhymes:
Their meals were plenteous, regular and plain;
The trade of Jonas brought him constant gain;
Vender of hops and malt, of coals and corn—
And, like his father, he was merchant born:
Neat was their house; each table, chair, and stool,
Stood in its place, or moving moved by rule;
No lively print or picture graced the room;
A plain brown paper lent its decent gloom;
But here the eye, in glancing round, survey'd
A small recess that seem'd for china made;

Such pleasing pictures seem'd this pencill'd ware,
That few would search for nobler objects there—
Yet, turn'd by chosen friends, and there appear'd
His stern, strong features, whom they all revered;
For there in lofty air was seen to stand
The bold Protector of the conquer'd land;
Drawn in that look with which he wept and swore,
Turn'd out the Members, and made fast the door,
Ridding the House of every knave and drone,
Forced, though it grieved his soul, to rule alone.
The stern still smile each friend approving gave,
Then turn'd the view, and all again were grave.[1]

There stood a clock, though small the owner's need,
For habit told when all things should proceed;
Few their amusements, but when friends appear'd,
They with the world's distress their spirits cheer'd;
The nation's guilt, that would not long endure
The reign of men so modest and so pure:
Their town was large, and seldom pass'd a day
But some had fail'd, and others gone astray;
Clerks had absconded, wives eloped, girls flown
To Gretna-Green, or sons rebellious grown;
Quarrels and fires arose;—and it was plain
The times were bad; the Saints had ceased to reign!
A few yet lived, to languish and to mourn
For good old manners never to return.

Jonas had sisters, and of these was one
Who lost a husband and an only son:
Twelve months her sables she in sorrow wore,
And mourn'd so long that she could mourn no more.

---

[1] Such was the actual consolation of a small knot of Presbyterians in
country town, about sixty years ago. (Note by Crabbe's son.)

Distant from Jonas, and from all her race,
She now resided in a lively place;
There, by the sect unseen, at whist she play'd,
Nor was of churchmen or their church afraid:
If much of this the graver brother heard,
He something censured, but he little fear'd;
He knew her rich and frugal; for the rest,
He felt no care, or, if he felt, suppress'd:
Nor for companion when she ask'd her Niece,
Had he suspicions that disturb'd his peace;
Frugal and rich, these virtues as a charm
Preserved the thoughtful man from all alarm;
An infant yet, she soon would home return,
Nor stay the manners of the world to learn;
Meantime his boys would all his care engross,
And be his comforts if he felt the loss.

The sprightly *Sybil*, pleased and unconfined,
Felt the pure pleasure of the op'ning mind:
All here was gay and cheerful—all at home
Unvaried quiet and unruffled gloom:
There were no changes, and amusements few;—
Here all was varied, wonderful, and new;
There were plain meals, plain dresses, and grave
    looks—
Here, gay companions and amusing books;
And the young Beauty soon began to taste
The light vocations of the scene she graced.

A man of business feels it as a crime
On calls domestic to consume his time;
Yet this grave man had not so cold a heart,
But with his daughter he was grieved to part:

And he demanded that in every year
The Aunt and Niece should at his house appear.

   'Yes! we must go, my child, and by our dress
'A grave conformity of mind express;
'Must sing at meeting, and from cards refrain,
'The more t' enjoy when we return again.'

   Thus spake the Aunt, and the discerning child
Was pleased to learn how fathers are beguiled.
Her artful part the young dissembler took,
And from the matron caught th' approving look:
When thrice the friends had met, excuse was sent
For more delay, and Jonas was content;
Till a tall maiden by her sire was seen,
In all the bloom and beauty of sixteen;
He gazed admiring;—she, with visage prim,
Glanced an arch look of gravity on him;
For she was gay at heart, but wore disguise,
And stood a vestal in her father's eyes:
Pure, pensive, simple, sad; the damsel's heart,
When Jonas praised, reproved her for the part;
For Sybil, fond of pleasure, gay and light,
Had still a secret bias to the right;
Vain as she was—and flattery made her vain—
Her simulation gave her bosom pain.

   Again return'd, the Matron and the Niece
Found the late quiet gave their joy increase;
The aunt infirm, no more her visits paid,
But still with her sojourn'd the favourite maid.
Letters were sent when franks could be procured,
And when they could not, silence was endured;

All were in health, and if they older grew,
It seem'd a fact that none among them knew;
The aunt and niece still led a pleasant life,
And quiet days had Jonas and his wife.

Near him a Widow dwelt of worthy fame,
Like his her manners, and her creed the same;
The wealth her husband left, her care retain'd
For one tall Youth, and widow she remain'd;
His love respectful all her care repaid,
Her wishes watch'd, and her commands obey'd.

Sober he was and grave from early youth,
Mindful of forms, but more intent on truth;
In a light drab he uniformly dress'd,
And look serene th' unruffled mind express'd;
A hat with ample verge his brows o'erspread,
And his brown locks curl'd graceful on his head;
Yet might observers in his speaking eye
Some observation, some acuteness spy;
The friendly thought it keen, the treacherous
    deem'd it sly;
Yet not a crime could foe or friend detect,
His actions all were, like his speech, correct;
And they who jested on a mind so sound,
Upon his virtues must their laughter found;
Chaste, sober, solemn, and devout they named
Him who was thus, and not of *this* ashamed.

Such were the virtues Jonas found in one
In whom he warmly wish'd to find a son:
Three years had pass'd since he had Sybil seen;
But she was doubtless what she once had been,

Lovely and mild, obedient and discreet;
The pair must love whenever they should meet;
Then ere the widow or her son should choose
Some happier maid, he would explain his views:
Now she, like him, was politic and shrewd,
With strong desire of lawful gain embued;
To all he said, she bow'd with much respect,
Pleased to comply, yet seeming to reject;
Cool and yet eager, each admired the strength
Of the opponent, and agreed at length:
As a drawn battle shows to each a force,
Powerful as his, he honours it of course;
So in these neighbours, each the power discern'd,
And gave the praise that was to each return'd.

Jonas now ask'd his daughter—and the Aunt,
Though loth to lose her, was obliged to grant:—
But would not Sybil to the matron cling,
And fear to leave the shelter of her wing?
No! in the young there lives a love of change,
And to the easy they prefer the strange!
Then, too, the joys she once pursued with zeal,
From whist and visits sprung, she ceased to feel:
When with the matrons Sybil first sat down,
To cut for partners and to stake her crown,
This to the youthful maid preferment seem'd,
Who thought what woman she was then
        esteem'd;
But in few years, when she perceived, indeed,
The real woman to the girl succeed,
No longer tricks and honours fill'd her mind,
But other feelings, not so well defined;

She then reluctant grew, and thought it hard
To sit and ponder o'er an ugly card;
Rather the nut-tree shade the nymph preferr'd,
Pleased with the pensive gloom and evening bird;
Thither, from company retired, she took
The silent walk, or read the fav'rite book.

The father's letter, sudden, short, and kind,
Awaked her wonder, and disturb'd her mind;
She found new dreams upon her fancy seize,
Wild roving thoughts and endless reveries:
The parting came;—and when the Aunt perceived
The tears of Sybil, and how much she grieved—
To love for her that tender grief she laid,
That various, soft, contending passions made.

When Sybil rested in her father's arms,
His pride exulted in a daughter's charms;
A maid accomplish'd he was pleased to find,
Nor seem'd the form more lovely than the mind:
But when the fit of pride and fondness fled,
He saw his judgment by his hopes misled;
High were the lady's spirits, far more free
Her mode of speaking than a maid's should be;
Too much, as Jonas thought, she seem'd to know,
And all her knowledge was disposed to show;
'Too gay her dress, like theirs who idly dote
'On a young coxcomb, or a coxcomb's coat;
'In foolish spirits when our friends appear,
'And vainly grave when not a man is near'.

Thus Jonas, adding to his sorrow blame,
And terms disdainful to a Sister's name:—

'The sinful wretch has by her arts defiled
'The ductile spirit of my darling child'.

'The maid is virtuous', said the dame—Quoth he
'Let her give proof, by acting virtuously:
'Is it in gaping when the Elders pray?
'In reading nonsense half a summer's day?
'In those mock forms that she delights to trace,
'Or her loud laughs in Hezekiah's face?
'She—O Susannah!—to the world belongs;
'She loves the follies of its idle throngs,
'And reads soft tales of love, and sings love's
        soft'ning songs.
'But, as our friend is yet delay'd in town,
'We must prepare her till the Youth comes down:
'You shall advise the maiden; I will threat;
'Her fears and hopes may yield us comfort yet'.

Now the grave father took the lass aside,
Demanding sternly, 'Wilt thou be a bride?'
She answer'd, calling up an air sedate,
'I have not vow'd against the holy state'.

'No folly, Sybil', said the parent; 'know
'What to their parents virtuous maidens owe:
'A worthy, wealthy youth, whom I approve,
'Must thou prepare to honour and to love.
'Formal to thee his air and dress may seem,
'But the good youth is worthy of esteem:
'Shouldst thou with rudeness treat him; of disdain
'Should he with justice or of slight complain,
'Or of one taunting speech give certain proof,
'Girl! I reject thee from my sober roof'.

80

'My aunt', said Sybil, 'will with pride protect
'One whom a father can for this reject;
'Nor shall a formal, rigid, soul-less boy
'My manners alter, or my views destroy!'

Jonas then lifted up his hands on high,
And, utt'ring something 'twixt a groan and sigh,
Left the determined maid, her doubtful mother by.

'Hear me', she said; 'incline thy heart, my child,
'And fix thy fancy on a man so mild:
'Thy father, Sybil, never could be moved
'By one who loved him, or by one he loved.
'Union like ours is but a bargain made
'By slave and tyrant—he will be obey'd;
'Then calls the quiet, comfort—but thy Youth
'Is mild by nature, and as frank as truth'.

'But will he love?' said Sybil; 'I am told
'That these mild creatures are by nature cold'.

'Alas!' the matron answer'd, 'much I dread
'That dangerous love by which the young are led!
'That love is earthy; you the creature prize,
'And trust your feelings and believe your eyes:
'Can eyes and feelings inward worth descry?
'No! my fair daughter, on our choice rely!
'Your love, like that display'd upon the stage,
'Indulged is folly, and opposed is rage;—
'More prudent love our sober couples show,
'All that to mortal beings, mortals owe;
'All flesh is grass—before you give a heart,
'Remember, Sybil, that in death you part;

'And should your husband die before your love,
'What needless anguish must a widow prove!
'No! my fair child, let all such visions cease;
'Yield but esteem, and only try for peace.'

  'I must be loved', said Sybil; 'I must see
'The man in terrors who aspires to me;
'At my forbidding frown his heart must ache,
'His tongue must falter, and his frame must shake:
'And if I grant him at my feet to kneel,
'What trembling, fearful pleasure must he feel;
'Nay, such the raptures that my smiles inspire,
'That reason's self must for a time retire'.

  'Alas! for good *Josiah*,' said the dame,
'These wicked thoughts would fill his soul with shame
'He kneel and tremble at a thing of dust!
'He cannot, child:'—the Child replied, 'He must'.

  They ceased: the matron left her with a frown;
So Jonas met her when the Youth came down:
'Behold,' said he, 'thy future spouse attends;
'Receive him, daughter, as the best of friends;
'Observe, respect him—humble be each word,
'That welcomes home thy husband and thy lord'.

  Forewarn'd, thought Sybil, with a bitter smile,
I shall prepare my manner and my style.

  Ere yet Josiah enter'd on his task,
The father met him—'Deign to wear a mask
'A few dull days, Josiah—but a few—
'It is our duty, and the sex's due;
'I wore it once, and every grateful wife
'Repays it with obedience through her life:

'Have no regard to Sybil's dress, have none
'To her pert language, to her flippant tone;
'Henceforward thou shalt rule unquestion'd and alone;
'And she thy pleasure in thy looks shall seek—
'How she shall dress, and whether she may speak'.

A sober smile return'd the Youth, and said,
'Can I cause fear, who am myself afraid?'

Sybil, meantime, sat thoughtful in her room,
And often wonder'd—'Will the creature come?
'Nothing shall tempt, shall force me to bestow
'My hand upon him,—yet I wish to know'.

The door unclosed, and she beheld her sire
Lead in the Youth, then hasten to retire;
'Daughter, my friend—my daughter, friend', he cried,
And gave a meaning look, and stepp'd aside:
That look contain'd a mingled threat and prayer,
'Do take him, child—offend him, if you dare'.

The couple gazed—were silent, and the maid
Look'd in his face, to make the man afraid;
The man, unmoved, upon the maiden cast
A steady view—so salutation pass'd:
But in this instant Sybil's eye had seen
The tall fair person, and the still staid mien;
The glow that temp'rance o'er the cheek had spread,
Where the soft down half veil'd the purest red;
And the serene deportment that proclaim'd
A heart unspotted, and a life unblamed:
But then with these she saw attire too plain,
The pale brown coat, though worn without a stain;

The formal air, and something of the pride
That indicates the wealth it seems to hide;
And looks that were not, she conceived, exempt
From a proud pity, or a sly contempt.

Josiah's eyes had their employment too,
Engaged and soften'd by so bright a view;
A fair and meaning face, an eye of fire,
That check'd the bold, and made the free retire:
But then with these he mark'd the studied dress
And lofty air, that scorn or pride express;
With that insidious look, that seem'd to hide
In an affected smile the scorn and pride;
And if his mind the virgin's meaning caught,
He saw a foe with treacherous purpose fraught—
Captive the heart to take, and to reject it, caught.

Silent they sat—thought Sybil, that he seeks
Something, no doubt; I wonder if he speaks:
Scarcely she wonder'd, when these accents fell
Slow in her ear—'Fair maiden, art thou well?'
'Art thou physician?' she replied; 'my hand,
'My pulse, at least, shall be at thy command'.

She said—and saw, surprised, Josiah kneel,
And gave his lips the offer'd pulse to feel;
The rosy colour rising in her cheek,
Seem'd that surprise unmix'd with wrath to speak;
Then sternness she assumed, and—'Doctor, tell;
'Thy words cannot alarm me—am I well?'

'Thou art', said he; 'and yet thy dress so light,
'I do conceive, some danger must excite':

'In whom?' said Sybil, with a look demure:
'In more', said he, 'than I expect to cure;—
'I, in thy light luxuriant robe, behold
'Want and excess, abounding and yet cold;
'Here needed, there display'd, in many a wanton fold:
'Both health and beauty, learned authors show,
'From a just medium in our clothing flow'.

　'Proceed, good doctor; if so great my need,
'What is thy fee? Good doctor! pray proceed.'

　'Large is my fee, fair lady, but I take
'None till some progress in my cure I make:
'Thou hast disease, fair maiden; thou art vain;
'Within that face sit insult and disdain;
'Thou art enamour'd of thyself; my art
'Can see the naughty malice of thy heart:
'With a strong pleasure would thy bosom move,
'Were I to own thy power, and ask thy love;
'And such thy beauty, damsel, that I might,
'But for thy pride, feel danger in thy sight,
'And lose my present peace in dreams of vain delight.'

　'And can thy patients', said the nymph, 'endure
'Physic like this? and will it work a cure?'

　'Such is my hope, fair damsel; thou, I find,
'Hast the true tokens of a noble mind;
'But the world wins thee, Sybil, and thy joys
'Are placed in trifles, fashions, follies, toys;
'Thou hast sought pleasure in the world around,
'That in thine own pure bosom should be found;
'Did all that world admire thee, praise and love,
'Could it the least of nature's pains remove?

85

'Could it for errors, follies, sins atone,
'Or give thee comfort, thoughtful and alone?
'It has, believe me, maid, no power to charm
'Thy soul from sorrow, or thy flesh from harm:
'Turn then, fair creature, from a world of sin,
'And seek the jewel happiness within.'

'Speak'st thou at meeting?' said the nymph; 'thy
        speech
'Is that of mortal very prone to teach;
'But wouldst thou, doctor, from the patient learn
'Thine own disease?—The cure is thy concern'.

'Yea, with good will.'—'Then know 't is thy
        complaint,
'That, for a sinner, thou 'rt too much a saint;
'Hast too much show of the sedate and pure,
'And without cause art formal and demure:
'This makes a man unsocial, unpolite;
'Odious when wrong, and insolent if right.
'Thou mayst be good, but why should goodness be
'Wrapt in a garb of such formality?
'Thy person well might please a damsel's eye,
'In decent habit with a scarlet dye;
'But, jest apart—what virtue canst thou trace
'In that broad brim that hides thy sober face?
'Does that long-skirted drab, that over-nice
'And formal clothing, prove a scorn of vice?
'Then for thine accent—what in sound can be
'So void of grace as dull monotony?
'Love has a thousand varied notes to move
'The human heart:—thou mayst not speak of love

86

'Till thou hast cast thy formal ways aside,
'And those becoming youth and nature tried:
'Not till exterior freedom, spirit, ease,
'Prove it thy study and delight to please;
'Not till these follies meet thy just disdain,
'While yet thy virtues and thy worth remain.'

   'This is severe!—Oh! maiden, wilt not thou
'Something for habits, manners, modes, allow?'—
'Yes! but allowing much, I much require,
'In my behalf, for manners, modes, attire!'

   'True, lovely Sybil; and, this point agreed,
'Let me to those of greater weight proceed:
'Thy father!'—'Nay,' she quickly interposed,
'Good doctor, here our conference is closed!'

   Then left the Youth, who, lost in his retreat,
Pass'd the good matron on her garden-seat;
His looks were troubled, and his air, once mild
And calm, was hurried:—'My audacious child!'
Exclaim'd the dame, 'I read what she has done
'In thy displeasure—Ah! the thoughtless one:
'But yet, Josiah, to my stern good man
'Speak of the maid as mildly as you can:
'Can you not seem to woo a little while
'The daughter's will, the father to beguile?
'So that his wrath in time may wear away;
'Will you preserve our peace, Josiah? say'.

   'Yes! my good neighbour,' said the gentle youth,
'Rely securely on my care and truth;
'And should thy comfort with my efforts cease,
'And only then,—perpetual is thy peace.'

87

The dame had doubts: she well his virtues knew,
His deeds were friendly, and his words were true:
'But to address this vixen is a task
'He is ashamed to take, and I to ask'.
Soon as the father from Josiah learn'd
What pass'd with Sybil, he the truth discern'd.
'He loves,' the man exclaim'd, 'he loves, 't is plain,
'The thoughtless girl, and shall he love in vain?
'She may be stubborn, but she shall be tried,
'Born as she is of wilfulness and pride.'

With anger fraught, but willing to persuade,
The wrathful father met the smiling maid:
'Sybil,' said he, 'I long, and yet I dread
'To know thy conduct—hath Josiah fled?
'And, grieved and fretted by thy scornful air,
'For his lost peace, betaken him to prayer?
'Couldst thou his pure and modest mind distress
'By vile remarks upon his speech, address,
'Attire, and voice?'—'All this I must confess.'
'Unhappy child! what labour will it cost
'To win him back!'—'I do not think him lost.'
'Courts he then (trifler!) insult and disdain?'—
'No; but from these he courts me to refrain.'
'Then hear me, Sybil: should Josiah leave
'Thy father's house?'—'My father's child would grieve.'
'That is of grace, and if he come again
'To speak of love?'—'I might from grief refrain.'
'Then wilt thou, daughter, our design embrace?'—
'Can I resist it, if it be of grace?'
'Dear child! in three plain words thy mind express:
'Wilt thou have this good youth?'—'Dear father! yes.'

THE WIDOW'S TALE

To Farmer *Moss*, in Langar Vale, came down,
His only Daughter, from her school in town;
A tender, timid maid! who knew not how
To pass a pig-sty, or to face a cow:
Smiling she came, with petty talents graced,
A fair complexion, and a slender waist.

Used to spare meals, disposed in manner pure,
Her father's kitchen she could ill endure:
Where by the steaming beef he hungry sat,
And laid at once a pound upon his plate;
Hot from the field, her eager brother seized
An equal part, and hunger's rage appeased;
The air surcharged with moisture, flagg'd around,
And the offended damsel sigh'd and frown'd;
The swelling fat in lumps conglomerate laid,
And fancy's sickness seized the loathing maid:
But when the men beside their station took,
The maidens with them, and with these the cook;
When one huge wooden bowl before them stood,
Fill'd with huge balls of farinaceous food;
With bacon, mass saline, where never lean
Beneath the brown and bristly rind was seen;
When from a single horn the party drew
Their copious draughts of heavy ale and new;
When the coarse cloth she saw, with many a stain
Soil'd by rude hinds who cut and came again—
She could not breathe; but with a heavy sigh,
Rein'd the fair neck, and shut th' offended eye;

She minced the sanguine flesh in frustums fine,
And wonder'd much to see the creatures dine.

*   *   *

LOVE'S BEGINNING

*   *   *

'At length 't was friendship—and my Friend and I
'Said we were happy, and began to sigh;
'My sisters first, and then my father, found
'That we were wandering o'er enchanted ground.'

*   *   *

TALE VIII

THE MOTHER

MARRIED LIFE

*   *   *

Here, on the favour'd beauty Fortune smiled;
Her chosen Husband was a man so mild,
So humbly temper'd, so intent to please,
It quite distress'd her to remain at ease,
Without a cause to sigh, without pretence to tease:
She tried his patience in a thousand modes,
And tired it not upon the roughest roads.
Pleasure she sought, and, disappointed, sigh'd
For joys, she said, 'to her alone denied';
And she was 'sure her parents, if alive,
'Would many comforts for their child contrive':
The gentle Husband bade her name him one;
'No—that', she answered, 'should for her be done;

'How could she say what pleasures were around?'
'But she was certain many might be found'.
'Would she some seaport, Weymouth, Scarborough,
    grace?'—
'He knew she hated every watering-place.'
'The town?'—'What! now 't was empty, joyless, dull?'
'In winter?'—'No; she liked it worse when full.'
She talk'd of building—'Would she plan a room?'—
'No! she could live, as he desired, in gloom.'
'Call then our friends and neighbours.'—'He might call,
'And they might come and fill his ugly hall;
'A noisy vulgar set, he knew she scorn'd them all.'
'Then might their two dear girls the time employ,
'And their improvement yield a solid joy.'—
'Solid indeed! and heavy—oh! the bliss
'Of teaching letters to a lisping miss!'
'My dear, my gentle Dorothea, say,
'Can I oblige you?'—'You may go away.'

  Twelve heavy years this patient soul sustain'd
This wasp's attacks, and then her praise obtain'd,
Graved on a marble tomb, where he at peace remain'd.

* * *

TALE IX

ARABELLA

Of a fair town where Doctor *Rack* was guide,
His only daughter was the boast and pride—
Wise *Arabella*, yet not wise alone,
She like a bright and polish'd brilliant shone;
Her father own'd her for his prop and stay,
Able to guide, yet willing to obey;

Pleased with her learning while discourse could
    please,
And with her love in languor and disease:
To every mother were her virtues known,
And to their daughters as a pattern shown;
Who in her youth had all that age requires,
And with her prudence all that youth admires:
These odious praises made the damsels try
Not to obtain such merits, but deny;
For, whatsoever wise mammas might say,
To guide a daughter, this was not the way;
From such applause disdain and anger rise,
And envy lives where emulation dies.
In all his strength, contends the noble horse
With one who just precedes him on the course;
But when the rival flies too far before,
His spirit fails, and he attempts no more.

This reasoning Maid, above her sex's dread,
Had dared to read, and dared to say she read;
Not the last novel, not the new-born play;
Not the mere trash and scandal of the day;
But (though her young companions felt the shock)
She studied Berkeley, Bacon, Hobbes, and Locke:
Her mind within the maze of history dwelt,
And of the moral Muse the beauty felt;
The merits of the Roman page she knew,
And could converse with More and Montague:
Thus she became the wonder of the town,
From that she reap'd, to that she gave renown;
And strangers coming, all were taught t' admire
The learned lady, and the lofty spire.

Thus Fame in public fix'd the Maid where all
Might throw their darts, and see the idol fall:
A hundred arrows came with vengeance keen,
From tongues envenom'd, and from arms unseen;
A thousand eyes were fix'd upon the place,
That, if she fell, she might not fly disgrace:
But malice vainly throws the poison'd dart,
Unless our frailty shows the peccant part;
And Arabella still preserved her name
Untouch'd, and shone with undisputed fame;
Her very notice some respect would cause,
And her esteem was honour and applause.

Men she avoided; not in childish fear,
As if she thought some savage foe was near;
Not as a prude, who hides that man should seek,
Or who by silence hints that they should speak;
But with discretion all the sex she view'd,
Ere yet engaged pursuing or pursued;
Ere love had made her to his vices blind,
Or hid the favourite's failings from her mind.

Thus was the picture of the man portray'd,
By merit destined for so rare a maid;
At whose request she might exchange her state,
Or still be happy in a virgin's fate:—
He must be one with manners like her own,
His life unquestion'd, his opinions known;
His stainless virtue must all tests endure,
His honour spotless, and his bosom pure;
She no allowance made for sex or times,
Of lax opinion—crimes were ever crimes;

No wretch forsaken must his frailty curse,
No spurious offspring drain his private purse:
He at all times his passions must command,
And yet possess—or be refused her hand.

All this without reserve the maiden told,
And some began to weigh the rector's gold;
To ask what sum a prudent man might gain,
Who had such store of virtues to maintain?

A Doctor *Campbell*, north of Tweed, came
      forth,
Declared his passion, and proclaim'd his worth;
Not unapproved, for he had much to say
On every cause, and in a pleasant way;
Not all his trust was in a pliant tongue,
His form was good, and ruddy he, and young:
But though the doctor was a man of parts,
He read not deeply male or female hearts;
But judged that all whom he esteem'd as wise
Must think alike, though some assumed disguise;
That every reasoning Bramin, Christian, Jew,
Of all religions took their liberal view;
And of her own, no doubt, this learned Maid
Denied the substance, and the forms obey'd:
And thus persuaded, he his thoughts express'd
Of her opinions, and his own profess'd:
'All states demand this aid, the vulgar need
'Their priests and pray'rs, their sermons and their
      creed;
'And those of stronger minds should never speak
'(In his opinion) what might hurt the weak:
'A man may smile, but still he should attend

'His hour at church, and be the Church's friend,
'What there he thinks conceal, and what he hears
    commend'.

Frank was the speech, but heard with high disdain,
Nor had the doctor leave to speak again;
A man who own'd, nay gloried in deceit,
'He might despise her, but he should not cheat'.

The Vicar *Holmes* appear'd: he heard it said
That ancient men best pleased the prudent maid;
And true it was her ancient friends she loved,
Servants when old she favour'd and approved;
Age in her pious parents she revered,
And neighbours were by length of days endear'd;
But, if her husband too must ancient be,
The good old vicar found it was not he.

On Captain *Bligh* her mind in balance hung—
Though valiant, modest; and reserved, though young:
Against these merits must defects be set—
Though poor, imprudent; and though proud, in debt:
In vain the captain close attention paid;
She found him wanting, whom she fairly weigh'd.

Then came a youth, and all their friends agreed
That *Edward Huntly* was the man indeed;
Respectful duty he had paid awhile,
Then ask'd her hand, and had a gracious smile:
A lover now declared, he led the fair
To woods and fields, to visits, and to pray'r;
Then whisper'd softly—'Will you name the day?'
She softly whisper'd—'If you love me, stay'.

'Oh! try me not beyond my strength', he cried:
'Oh! be not weak,' the prudent Maid replied;
'But by some trial your affection prove—
'Respect, and not impatience, argues love:
'And love no more is by impatience known,
'Than ocean's depth is by its tempests shown:
'He whom a weak and fond impatience sways,
'But for himself with all his fervour prays,
'And not the maid he woos, but his own will obeys;
'And will she love the being who prefers,
'With so much ardour, his desire to hers?'

Young Edward grieved, but let not grief be seen;
He knew obedience pleased his fancy's queen:
Awhile he waited, and then cried—'Behold!
'The year advancing, be no longer cold!'
For she had promised—'Let the flowers appear,
'And I will pass with thee the smiling year':
Then pressing grew the youth; the more he press'd,
The less inclined the maid to his request:
'Let June arrive'.—Alas! when April came,
It brought a stranger, and the stranger, shame;
Nor could the Lover from his house persuade
A stubborn lass whom he had mournful made;
Angry and weak, by thoughtless vengeance moved,
She told her story to the Fair beloved;
In strongest words th' unwelcome truth was shown,
To blight his prospects, careless of her own.

Our heroine grieved, but had too firm a heart
For him to soften, when she swore to part;
In vain his seeming penitence and pray'r,
His vows, his tears; she left him in despair:

His mother fondly laid her grief aside,
And to the reason of the nymph applied.—

    'It well becomes thee, lady, to appear,
'But not to be, in very truth, severe;
'Although the crime be odious in thy sight,
'That daring sex is taught such things to slight:
'His heart is thine, although it once was frail;
'Think of his grief, and let his love prevail!'

    'Plead thou no more', the lofty lass return'd:
'Forgiving woman is deceived and spurn'd:
'Say that the crime is common—shall I take
'A common man my wedded lord to make?
'See! a weak woman by his arts betray'd,
'An infant born his father to upbraid;
'Shall I forgive his vileness, take his name,
'Sanction his error, and partake his shame?
'No! this assent would kindred frailty prove,
'A love for him would be a vicious love:
'Can a chaste maiden secret counsel hold
'With one whose crime by every mouth is told?
'Forbid it spirit, prudence, virtuous pride;
'He must despise me, were he not denied:
'The way from vice the erring mind to win
'Is with presuming sinners to begin,
'And show, by scorning them, a just contempt for sin.'

    The youth, repulsed, to one more mild convey'd
His heart, and smiled on the remorseless maid;
The maid, remorseless in her pride, the while
Despised the insult, and return'd the smile.

First to admire, to praise her, and defend,
Was (now in years advanced) a virgin-friend:
Much she preferr'd, she cried, the single state,
'It was her choice'—it surely was her fate;
And much it pleased her in the train to view
A maiden vot'ress, wise and lovely too.

Time to the yielding mind his change imparts,
He varies notions, and he alters hearts;
'T is right, 't is just to feel contempt for vice,
But he that shows it may be over-nice:
There are who feel, when young, the false sublime,
And proudly love to show disdain for crime;
To whom the future will new thoughts supply,
The pride will soften, and the scorn will die;
Nay, where they still the vice itself condemn,
They bear the vicious, and consort with them:
Young Captain Grove, when one had changed his
    side,
Despised the venal turncoat, and defied;
Old Colonel Grove now shakes him by the hand,
Though he who bribes may still his vote command.
Why would not Ellen to Belinda speak,
When she had flown to London for a week,
And then return'd, to every friend's surprise,
With twice the spirit, and with half the size?
She spoke not then—but, after years had flown,
A better friend had Ellen never known:
Was it the lady her mistake had seen?
Or had she also such a journey been?
No: 't was the gradual change in human hearts,
That time, in commerce with the world, imparts;

That on the roughest temper throws disguise,
And steals from virtue her asperities.
The young and ardent, who with glowing zeal
Felt wrath for trifles, and were proud to feel,
Now find those trifles all the mind engage,
To soothe dull hours, and cheat the cares of age;
As young Zelinda, in her quaker-dress,
Disdain'd each varying fashion's vile excess,
And now her friends on old Zelinda gaze,
Pleased in rich silks and orient gems to blaze:
Changes like these 't is folly to condemn,
So virtue yields not, nor is changed with them.

    Let us proceed:—Twelve brilliant years were
        past,
Yet each with less of glory than the last.
Whether these years to this fair virgin gave
A softer mind—effect they often have;
Whether the virgin-state was not so bless'd
As that good maiden in her zeal profess'd;
Or whether lovers falling from her train,
Gave greater price to those she could retain,
Is all unknown;—but Arabella now
Was kindly listening to a Merchant's vow,
Who offer'd terms so fair, against his love
To strive was folly, so she never strove.—
Man in his earlier days we often find
With a too easy and unguarded mind;
But by increasing years and prudence taught,
He grows reserved, and locks up every thought:
Not thus the maiden, for in blooming youth
She hides her thought and guards the tender truth:

This, when no longer young, no more she hides,
But frankly in the favour'd swain confides:
Man, stubborn man, is like the growing tree,
That, longer standing, still will harder be;
And like its fruit, the virgin, first austere,
Then kindly softening with the ripening year.

Now was the lover urgent, and the kind
And yielding lady to his suit inclined:
'A little time, my friend, is just, is right;
'We must be decent in our neighbours' sight':
Still she allow'd him of his hopes to speak,
And in compassion took off week by week;
Till few remain'd, when, wearied with delay,
She kindly meant to take off day by day.

That female Friend who gave our virgin praise
For flying man and all his treacherous ways,
Now heard with mingled anger, shame, and fear,
Of one accepted, and a wedding near;
But she resolved again with friendly zeal
To make the maid her scorn of wedlock feel;
For she was grieved to find her work undone,
And like a sister mourn'd the failing nun.

Why are these gentle maidens prone to make
Their sister-doves the tempting world forsake?
Why all their triumph when a maid disdains
The tyrant sex, and scorns to wear its chains?
Is it pure joy to see a sister flown
From the false pleasures they themselves have known?
Or do they, as the call-birds in the cage,
Try, in pure envy, others to engage?

And therefore paint their native woods and groves,
As scenes of dangerous joys and naughty loves?

Strong was the maiden's hope; her friend was proud,
And had her notions to the world avow'd;
And, could she find the Merchant weak and frail,
With power to prove it, then she must prevail:
For she aloud would publish his disgrace,
And save his victim from a man so base.

When all inquiries had been duly made,
Came the kind Friend her burthen to unlade:—
'Alas! my dear! not all our care and art
'Can thread the maze of man's deceitful heart:
'Look not surprise—nor let resentment swell
'Those lovely features, all will yet be well;
'And thou, from love's and man's deceptions free,
'Wilt dwell in virgin-state, and walk to Heaven with
    me'.

The Maiden frown'd, and then conceived 'that wives
'Could walk as well, and lead as holy lives,
'As angry prudes who scorn'd the marriage-chain,
'Or luckless maids, who sought it still in vain'.

The Friend was vex'd—she paused: at length she
    cried,
'Know your own danger, then your lot decide:
'That traitor Beswell, while he seeks your hand,
'Has, I affirm, a wanton at command;
'A slave, a creature from a foreign place,
'The nurse and mother of a spurious race;
'Brown ugly bastards (Heaven the word forgive,
'And the deed punish!) in his cottage live;

'To town if business calls him, there he stays
'In sinful pleasures wasting countless days.
'Nor doubt the facts, for I can witness call,
'For every crime, and prove them one and all'.

Here ceased th' informer; Arabella's look
Was like a schoolboy's puzzled by his book;
Intent she cast her eyes upon the floor,
Paused—then replied—
     'I wish to know no more:
'I question not your motive, zeal, or love,
'But must decline such dubious points to prove.
'All is not true, I judge, for who can guess
'Those deeds of darkness men with care suppress?
'He brought a slave perhaps to England's coast,
'And made her free; it is our country's boast!
'And she perchance too grateful—good and ill
'Were sown at first, and grow together still;
'The colour'd infants on the village green,
'What are they more than we have often seen?
'Children half-clothed who round their village stray,
'In sun or rain, now starved, now beaten, they
'Will the dark colour of their fate betray:
'Let us in Christian love for all account,
'And then behold to what such tales amount'.

'His heart is evil', said the impatient Friend:
'My duty bids me try that heart to mend',
Replied the virgin; 'we may be too nice
'And lose a soul in our contempt of vice;
'If false the charge, I then shall show regard
'For a good man, and be his just reward:

102

'And what for virtue can I better do
'Than to reclaim him, if the charge be true?'

She spoke, nor more her holy work delay'd;
'T was time to lend an erring mortal aid:
'The noblest way', she judged, 'a soul to win,
'Was with an act of kindness to begin,
'To make the sinner sure, and then t' attack the sin'.

TALE X

THE LOVER'S JOURNEY

It is the Soul that sees: the outward eyes
Present the object, but the Mind descries;
And thence delight, disgust, or cool indiff'rence rise:
When minds are joyful, then we look around,
And what is seen is all on fairy ground;
Again they sicken, and on every view
Cast their own dull and melancholy hue;
Or, if absorb'd by their peculiar cares,
The vacant eye on viewless matter glares,
Our feelings still upon our views attend,
And their own natures to the objects lend:
Sorrow and joy are in their influence sure,
Long as the passion reigns th' effects endure;
But Love in minds his various changes makes,
And clothes each object with the change he takes;
His light and shade on every view he throws,
And on each object what he feels bestows.

Fair was the morning, and the month was June,
When rose a Lover;—love awakens soon:

Brief his repose, yet much he dreamt the while
Of that day's meeting, and his *Laura's* smile:
Fancy and love that name assign'd to her,
Call'd Susan in the parish-register;
And he no more was John—his Laura gave
The name *Orlando* to her faithful slave.

Bright shone the glory of the rising day,
When the fond traveller took his favourite way;
He mounted gaily, felt his bosom light,
And all he saw was pleasing in his sight.

'Ye hours of expectation, quickly fly,
'And bring on hours of bless'd reality;
'When I shall Laura see, beside her stand,
'Hear her sweet voice, and press her yielded hand.'

First o'er a barren heath beside the coast
Orlando rode, and joy began to boast.

'This neat low gorse,' said he, 'with golden bloom,
'Delights each sense, is beauty, is perfume;
'And this gay ling, with all its purple flowers,
'A man at leisure might admire for hours;
'This green-fringed cup-moss has a scarlet tip,
'That yields to nothing but my Laura's lip;
'And then how fine this herbage! men may say
'A heath is barren; nothing is so gay:
'Barren or bare to call such charming scene
'Argues a mind possess'd by care and spleen.'

Onward he went, and fiercer grew the heat,
Dust rose in clouds before the horse's feet;
For now he pass'd through lanes of burning sand,
Bounds to thin crops or yet uncultured land;

Where the dark poppy flourish'd on the dry
And sterile soil, and mock'd the thin-set rye.

'How lovely this!' the rapt Orlando said;
'With what delight is labouring man repaid!
'The very lane has sweets that all admire,
'The rambling suckling, and the vigorous brier;
'See! wholesome wormwood grows beside the way,
'Where dew-press'd yet the dog-rose bends the spray;
'Fresh herbs the fields, fair shrubs the banks adorn,
'And snow-white bloom falls flaky from the thorn;
'No fostering hand they need, no sheltering wall,
'They spring uncultured, and they bloom for all.'

The Lover rode as hasty lovers ride,
And reach'd a common pasture wild and wide;
Small black-legg'd sheep devour with hunger keen
The meagre herbage, fleshless, lank, and lean:
Such o'er thy level turf, Newmarket! stray,
And there, with other *black-legs*[1], find their prey.
He saw some scatter'd hovels; turf was piled
In square brown stacks; a prospect bleak and wild!
A mill, indeed, was in the centre found,
With short sear herbage withering all around;
A smith's black shed opposed a wright's long shop,
And join'd an inn where humble travellers stop.

'Ay, this is Nature', said the gentle 'Squire;
'This ease, peace, pleasure—who would not admire?
'With what delight these sturdy children play,
'And joyful rustics at the close of day;
'Sport follows labour; on this even space
'Will soon commence the wrestling and the race;

[1] Sharpers.

105

'Then will the village-maidens leave their home,
'And to the dance with buoyant spirits come;
'No affectation in their looks is seen,
'Nor know they what disguise or flattery mean;
'Nor aught to move an envious pang they see,
'Easy their service, and their love is free;
'Hence early springs that love, it long endures,
'And life's first comfort, while they live, ensures:
'They the low roof and rustic comforts prize,
'Nor cast on prouder mansions envying eyes:
'Sometimes the news at yonder town they hear,
'And learn what busier mortals feel and fear;
'Secure themselves, although by tales amazed
'Of towns bombarded and of cities razed;
'As if they doubted, in their still retreat,
'The very news that makes their quiet sweet,
'And their days happy—happier only knows
'He on whom Laura her regard bestows.'

On rode Orlando, counting all the while
The miles he pass'd, and every coming mile;
Like all attracted things, he quicker flies,
The place approaching where th' attraction lies;
When next appear'd a *dam*—so call the place—
Where lies a road confined in narrow space;
A work of labour, for on either side
Is level fen, a prospect wild and wide,
With dikes on either hand by ocean's self supplied:
Far on the right the distant sea is seen,
And salt the springs that feed the marsh between;
Beneath an ancient bridge, the straiten'd flood
Rolls through its sloping banks of slimy mud;

Near it a sunken boat resists the tide,
That frets and hurries to th' opposing side;
The rushes sharp, that on the borders grow,
Bend their brown flow'rets to the stream below,
Impure in all its course, in all its progress slow.

*   *   *

Here on its wiry stem, in rigid bloom,
Grows the salt lavender that lacks perfume;
Here the dwarf sallows creep, the septfoil harsh,
And the soft slimy mallow of the marsh;
Low on the ear the distant billows sound,
And just in view appears their stony bound;
No hedge nor tree conceals the glowing sun,
Birds, save a wat'ry tribe, the district shun,
Nor chirp among the reeds where bitter waters run.

  'Various as beauteous, Nature, is thy face',
Exclaim'd Orlando: 'all that grows has grace:
'All are appropriate—bog, and marsh, and fen,
'Are only poor to undiscerning men;
'Here may the nice and curious eye explore
'How Nature's hand adorns the rushy moor;
'Here the rare moss in secret shade is found,
'Here the sweet myrtle of the shaking ground;
'Beauties are these that from the view retire,
'But well repay th' attention they require;
'For these my Laura will her home forsake,
'And all the pleasures they afford partake'.

  Again, the country was enclosed, a wide
And sandy road has banks on either side;

Where, lo! a hollow on the left appear'd,
And there a gipsy tribe their tent had rear'd;
'T was open spread, to catch the morning sun,
And they had now their early meal begun,
When two brown boys just left their grassy seat,
The early Trav'ller with their prayers to greet:
While yet Orlando held his pence in hand,
He saw their sister on her duty stand;
Some twelve years old, demure, affected, sly,
Prepared the force of early powers to try;
Sudden a look of languor he descries,
And well-feign'd apprehension in her eyes;
Train'd but yet savage, in her speaking face
He mark'd the features of her vagrant race;
When a light laugh and roguish leer express'd
The vice implanted in her youthful breast:
Forth from the tent her elder brother came,
Who seem'd offended, yet forbore to blame
The young designer, but could only trace
The looks of pity in the Trav'ller's face:
Within, the Father, who from fences nigh
Had brought the fuel for the fire's supply,
Watch'd now the feeble blaze, and stood
        dejected by.
On ragged rug, just borrow'd from the bed,
And by the hand of coarse indulgence fed,
In dirty patchwork negligently dress'd,
Reclined the Wife, an infant at her breast;
In her wild face some touch of grace remain'd,
Of vigour palsied and of beauty stain'd;
Her bloodshot eyes on her unheeding mate
Were wrathful turn'd, and seem'd her wants to state,

Cursing his tardy aid—her Mother there
With gipsy-state engross'd the only chair;
Solemn and dull her look; with such she stands,
And reads the milk-maid's fortune in her hands,
Tracing the lines of life; assumed through years,
Each feature now the steady falsehood wears:
With hard and savage eye she views the food,
And grudging pinches their intruding brood;
Last in the group, the worn-out Grandsire sits
Neglected, lost, and living but by fits:
Useless, despised, his worthless labours done,
And half protected by the vicious Son,
Who half supports him; he with heavy glance
Views the young ruffians who around him dance;
And, by the sadness in his face, appears
To trace the progress of their future years:
Through what strange course of misery, vice,
        deceit,
Must wildly wander each unpractised cheat!
What shame and grief, what punishment and pain,
Sport of fierce passions, must each child sustain—
Ere they like him approach their latter end,
Without a hope, a comfort, or a friend!

But this Orlando felt not; 'Rogues,' said he,
'Doubtless they are, but merry rogues they be;
'They wander round the land, and be it true
'They break the laws—then let the laws pursue
'The wanton idlers; for the life they live,
'Acquit I cannot, but I can forgive'.
This said, a portion from his purse was thrown,
And every heart seem'd happy like his own.

He hurried forth, for now the town was nigh—
'The happiest man of mortal men am I'.
Thou art! but change in every state is near
(So while the wretched hope, the bless'd may fear):
'Say, where is Laura?'—'That her words must show',
A lass replied; 'read this, and thou shalt know!'

'What, gone!—"Her friend insisted—forced to go:—
'"Is vex'd, was teased, could not refuse her!"—No?
'"But you can follow." Yes! "The miles are few,
'"The way is pleasant; will you come?—Adieu!
'"Thy Laura!" No! I feel I must resign
'The pleasing hope; thou hadst been here, if mine.
'A lady was it?—Was no brother there?
'But why should I afflict me, if there were?
'"The way is pleasant." What to me the way?
'I cannot reach her till the close of day.
'My dumb companion! is it thus we speed?
'Not I from grief nor thou from toil art freed;
'Still art thou doom'd to travel and to pine,
'For my vexation—What a fate is mine!

'Gone to a friend, she tells me;—I commend
'Her purpose: means she to a female friend?
'By Heaven, I wish she suffer'd half the pain
'Of hope protracted through the day in vain.
'Shall I persist to see th' ungrateful maid?
'Yes, I will see her, slight her, and upbraid.
'What! in the very hour? She knew the time,
'And doubtless chose it to increase her crime.'

Forth rode Orlando by a river's side,
Inland and winding, smooth, and full, and wide,
That roll'd majestic on, in one soft-flowing tide;

The bottom gravel, flow'ry were the banks,
Tall willows waving in their broken ranks;
The road, now near, now distant, winding led
By lovely meadows which the waters fed;
He pass'd the way-side inn, the village spire,
Nor stopp'd to gaze, to question, or admire;
On either side the rural mansions stood,
With hedge-row trees, and hills high-crown'd
    with wood,
And many a devious stream that reach'd the
    nobler flood.

  'I hate these scenes,' Orlando angry cried,
'And these proud farmers! yes, I hate their pride.
'See! that sleek fellow, how he strides along,
'Strong as an ox, and ignorant as strong;
'Can yon close crops a single eye detain
'But he who counts the profits of the grain?
'And these vile beans with deleterious smell,
'Where is their beauty? can a mortal tell?
'These deep fat meadows I detest; it shocks
'One's feelings there to see the grazing ox;—
'For slaughter fatted, as a lady's smile
'Rejoices man, and means his death the while.
'Lo! now the sons of labour! every day
'Employ'd in toil, and vex'd in every way;
'Theirs is but mirth assumed, and they conceal,
'In their affected joys, the ills they feel:
'I hate these long green lanes; there's nothing seen
'In this vile country but eternal green;
'Woods! waters! meadows! Will they never end?
''T is a vile prospect:—Gone to see a friend!'

Still on he rode! a mansion fair and tall
Rose on his view—the pride of Loddon Hall:
Spread o'er the park he saw the grazing steer,
The full-fed steed, and herds of bounding deer:
On a clear stream the vivid sunbeams play'd,
Through noble elms, and on the surface made
That moving picture, checker'd light and shade;
Th' attended children, there indulged to stray,
Enjoy'd and gave new beauty to the day;
Whose happy parents from their room were seen
Pleased with the sportive idlers on the green.

'Well!' said Orlando, 'and for one so bless'd,
'A thousand reasoning wretches are distress'd;
'Nay, these, so seeming glad, are grieving like the
    rest:
'Man is a cheat—and all but strive to hide
'Their inward misery by their outward pride.
'What do yon lofty gates and walls contain,
'But fruitless means to soothe unconquer'd pain?
'The parents read each infant daughter's smile,
'Form'd to seduce, encouraged to beguile;
'They view the boys unconscious of their fate,
'Sure to be tempted, sure to take the bait;
'These will be Lauras, sad Orlandos these—
'There 's guilt and grief in all one hears and sees.'

Our Trav'ller, lab'ring up a hill, look'd down
Upon a lively, busy, pleasant town;
All he beheld were there alert, alive,
The busiest bees that ever stock'd a hive:
A pair were married, and the bells aloud
Proclaim'd their joy, and joyful seem'd the crowd;

112

And now, proceeding on his way, he spied,
Bound by strong ties, the bridegroom and the bride;
Each by some friends attended, near they drew,
And spleen beheld them with prophetic view.

'Married! nay, mad!' Orlando cried in scorn;
'Another wretch on this unlucky morn:
'What are this foolish mirth, these idle joys?
'Attempts to stifle doubt and fear by noise:
'To me these robes, expressive of delight,
'Foreshow distress, and only grief excite;
'And for these cheerful friends, will they behold
'Their wailing brood in sickness, want, and cold;
'And his proud look, and her soft languid air
'Will—but I spare you—go, unhappy pair!'

And now, approaching to the Journey's end,
His anger fails, his thoughts to kindness tend,
He less offended feels, and rather fears t' offend:
Now gently rising, hope contends with doubt,
And casts a sunshine on the views without;
And still reviving joy and lingering gloom
Alternate empire o'er his soul assume;
Till, long perplex'd, he now began to find
The softer thoughts engross the settling mind:
He saw the mansion, and should quickly see
His Laura's self—and angry could he be?
No! the resentment melted all away—
'For this my grief a single smile will pay,'
Our trav'ller cried;—'And why should it offend,
'That one so good should have a pressing friend?
'Grieve not, my heart! to find a favourite guest

'Thy pride and boast—ye selfish sorrows, rest;
'She will be kind, and I again be bless'd'.

While gentler passions thus his bosom sway'd,
He reach'd the mansion, and he saw the maid;
'My Laura!'—'My Orlando!—this is kind;
'In truth I came persuaded, not inclined:
'Our friends' amusement let us now pursue,
'And I to-morrow will return with you.'

Like man entranced the happy Lover stood—
'As Laura wills, for she is kind and good;
'Ever the truest, gentlest, fairest, best—
'As Laura wills: I see her and am bless'd.'

Home went the Lovers through that busy place,
By Loddon Hall, the country's pride and grace;
By the rich meadows where the oxen fed,
Through the green vale that form'd the river's bed;
And by unnumber'd cottages and farms,
That have for musing minds unnumber'd charms;
And how affected by the view of these
Was then Orlando?—did they pain or please?

Nor pain nor pleasure could they yield—and why?
The mind was fill'd, was happy, and the eye
Roved o'er the fleeting views, that but appear'd to die.

Alone Orlando on the morrow paced
The well-known road; the gipsy-tent he traced;
The dam high-raised, the reedy dykes between,
The scatter'd hovels on the barren green,
The burning sand, the fields of thin-set rye,
Mock'd by the useless Flora, blooming by;

And last the heath with all its various bloom,
And the close lanes that led the trav'ller home.

Then could these scenes the former joys renew?
Or was there now dejection in the view?—
Nor one or other would they yield—and why?
The mind was absent, and the vacant eye
Wander'd o'er viewless scenes, that but appear'd
   to die.

TALE XII

'SQUIRE THOMAS; OR, THE
PRECIPITATE CHOICE

'Squire Thomas flatter'd long a wealthy Aunt,
Who left him all that she could give or grant;
Ten years he tried, with all his craft and skill,
To fix the sovereign lady's varying will;
Ten years enduring at her board to sit,
He meekly listen'd to her tales and wit:
He took the meanest office man can take,
And his aunt's vices for her money's sake:
By many a threat'ning hint she waked his fear,
And he was pain'd to see a rival near:
Yet all the taunts of her contemptuous pride
He bore, nor found his grov'ling spirit tried;
Nay, when she wish'd his parents to traduce,
Fawning he smiled, and justice call'd th' abuse:
'They taught you nothing: are you not, at best',
Said the proud Dame, 'a trifler, and a jest?
'Confess you are a fool!'—he bow'd and he confess'd.

This vex'd him much, but could not always last:
The dame is buried, and the trial past.

There was a female, who had courted long
Her cousin's gifts, and deeply felt the wrong;
By a vain boy forbidden to attend
The private councils of her wealthy friend,
She vow'd revenge, nor should that crafty boy
In triumph undisturb'd his spoils enjoy:
He heard, he smiled, and when the Will was read
Kindly dismiss'd the Kindred of the dead;
'The dear deceased' he call'd her, and the crowd
Moved off with curses deep and threat'nings loud.

*   *   *

FLIRTATION

A DIALOGUE

FROM her own room, in summer's softest eve,
Stepp'd *Celia* forth her *Delia* to receive,—
Joy in her looks, that half her tale declared.

C. War and the waves my fav'rite Youth have spared;
Faithful and fond, through many a painful year,
My Charles will come——Do give me joy, my dear.

D. I give you joy, and so may he; but still,
'T is right to question if 't is sure he will;
A sailor's open honest heart we prize,
But honest sailors have their ears and eyes.

C. Oh! but he surely will on me depend,
Nor dare to doubt the firmness of his friend.

D. Be not secure; the very best have foes,
And facts they would not to the world expose;
And these he may be told, if he converse with those.

C. Speak you in friendship?—let it be sincere
And naked truth,—and what have I to fear?

D. I speak in friendship; and I do confess,
If I were you, the Truth should wear a dress:
If Charles should doubt, as lovers do, though blind,
Would you to him present the naked mind?
If it were clear as crystal, yet it checks
One's joy to think that he may fancy specks;
And now, in five long years, we scarcely know
How the mind gets them, and how large they grow.
Let woman be as rigid as a nun,
She cannot censures and surmises shun.
Wonder not, then, at tales that Scandal tells—
Your father's rooms were not like sisters' cells;
Nor pious monks came there, nor prosing friars,
But well-dress'd captains and approving squires.

C. What these to me, admit th' account be true?

D. Nay, that yourself describe—they came to you!

C. Well! to my friend I may the truth confess,
Poor Captain Glimmer loved me to excess;
Flintham, the young solicitor, that wrote
Those pretty verses, he began to dote;
That Youth from Oxford, when I used to stop
A moment with him, at my feet would drop;
Nor less your Brother, whom, for your dear sake,
I to my favour often used to take:
And was, vile world! my character at stake?

If such reports my Sailor's ear should reach,
What jealous thoughts and fancies may they teach!
If without cause ill-judging men suspect,
What may not all these harmless truths effect?
And what, my Delia, if our virtues fail,
What must we fear if conscious we are frail?
And well you know, my friend, nor fear t' impart,
The tender frailties of the yielding heart.

D. Speak for yourself, fair lady! speak with care;
I, not your frailties, but your suffering share:
You may my counsel, if you will, refuse;
But pray beware how you my name accuse.

C. Accuse you! No! there is no need of one
To do what long the public voice has done!
What misses then at school forget the fall
Of Ensign Bloomer when he leap'd the wall?
That was a first exploit, and we were witness all;
And that sad night, upon my faithful breast,
We wept together till we sank to rest;
You own'd your love——

    D. A girl, a chit, a child!
Am I for this, and by a friend, reviled?

C. Then lay your hand, fair creature! on your heart,
And say how many there have had a part:
Six I remember; and, if Fame be true,
The handsome Serjeant had his portion too.

D. A Serjeant! Madam, if I might advise,
Do use some small discretion in such lies:
A Serjeant, Celia?——

C. Handsome, smart, and clean.
Yes! and the fellow had a noble mien,
That might excuse you had you giv'n your hand,—
But this your father could not understand.

D. Mercy! how pert and flippant are you grown,
As if you 'd not a secret of your own!
Yet would you tremble should your Sailor know
What I or my small cabinet could show:
He might suspect a heart with many a wound,
Shallow and deep, could never more be sound;
That of one pierced so oft, so largely bled,
The feeling ceases and the love is dead;
But sense exists, and passion serves instead.

C. Injurious Delia! cold, reproachful maid!
Is thus my confidential faith repaid?
Is this the counsel that we two have held
When duty trembled and desire rebell'd;
The sister-vows we made, through many a night,
To aid each other in the arduous fight
With the harsh-minded powers who never think
What nature needs, nor will at weakness wink?
And now, thou cruel girl! is all forgot,
The wish oft whisper'd, the imagined lot,
The secret Hymen, the sequester'd cot?
And will you thus our bond of friendship rend,
And join the world in censure of your friend?
Oh! 't is not right! as all with scorn must see,
Although the certain mischief falls on me.

D. Nay, never weep! but let this kiss restore,
And make our friendship perfect as before;

Do not our wiser selves ourselves condemn?
And yet we dearly love their faults and them.
So our reproofs to tender minds are shown,
We treat their wanderings as we treat our own;
We are each other's conscience, and we tell
Our friend her fault, because we wish her well;
We judge, nay prejudge, what may be her case,
Fore-arm the soul, and shield her from disgrace.
Creatures in prison, ere the trying day,
Their answers practise, and their powers essay.
By means like these they guard against surprise,
And all the puzzling questions that may rise.

'Guilty or not?' His lawyer thus address'd
A wealthy rogue. 'Not guilty, I protest.'
'Why, then, my friend, we've nothing here to say,
'But you're in danger! prithee heed your way:
'*You* know your truth, *I* where your error lies:
'From your "*Not* guilty" will your danger rise.'
'Oh! but I *am*, and I have here the gain
'Of wicked craft.'—'Then let it *here* remain;
'For we must guard it by a sure defence,
'And not professions of your innocence;
'For that's the way, whatever you suppose,
'To slip your neck within the ready noose.'

Thus, my beloved friend, a girl, if wise,
Upon her Prudence, not her Truth, relies.
It is confess'd, that not the good and pure
Are in this world of calumny secure;
And therefore never let a lass rely
Upon her goodness and her chastity:

Her very virtue makes her heedless: youth
Reveals imprudent, nay injurious, truth;
Whereas, if conscious that she merit blame,
She grows discreet, and well defends her fame;
And thus, offending, better makes her way—
As Joseph Surface argues in the play—
Than when in virtue's strength she proudly stood,
So wrongly right, and so absurdly good.

Now, when your Charles shall be your judge, and try
His own dear damsel—questioning how and why—
Let her be ready, arm'd with prompt reply;
No hesitation let the man discern,
But answer boldly, then accuse in turn;
Some trifling points with candid speech confess'd,
You gain a monstrous credit for the rest.
Then may you wear the Injured Lady frown,
And with your anger keep his malice down;
Accuse, condemn, and make him glad at heart
To sue for pardon when you come to part;
But let him have it; let him go in peace,
And all inquiries of themselves will cease;
To touch him nearer, and to hold him fast,
Have a few tears *in petto* at the last;
But, this with care! for 't is a point of doubt,
If you should end with weeping or without.
'T is true you much affect him by your pain,
But he may want to prove his power again;
And, then, it spoils the look, and hurts the eyes—
A girl is never handsome when she cries.
Take it for granted, in a general way,
The more you weep for men, the more you may.

Save your resources; for though now you cry
With good effect, you may not by and by.
It is a knack; and there are those that weep
Without emotion that a man may sleep;
Others disgust—'t is genius, not advice,
That will avail us in a thing so nice.
If you should love him, you have greater need
Of all your care, and may not then succeed:—
For that 's our bane—we should be conquerors all
With hearts untouch'd—our feelings cause our fall.
But your experience aids you: you can hide
Your real weakness in your borrow'd pride.

But to the point: should so the Charge be laid,
That nought against it fairly can be said—
How would you act? You would not then confess?

C. Oh! never! no!—nor even my Truth profess!
To mute contempt I would alone resort
For the Reporters, and for their Report.
If he profess'd forgiveness, I would cry—
'Forgive such faithlessness! so would not I.
'Such errors pardon! he that so would act
'Would, I am sure, be guilty of the fact;
'Charles, if I thought your spirit was so mean,
'I would not longer in your walks be seen:
'Could you such woman for a moment prize?
'You might forgive her, but you must despise'.

D. Bravo, my girl! 't is then our sex command,
When we can seize the weapon in their hand,
When we their charge so manage, that 't is found
To save the credit it was meant to wound.

122

Those who by reasons their acquittal seek,
Make the whole sex contemptible and weak;
This, too, observe—that men of sense in love
Dupes more complete than fools and blockheads prove;
For all that knowledge, lent them as a guide,
Goes off entirely to the lady's side;
Whereas the blockhead rather sees the more,
And gains perception that he lack'd before.
His honest passion blinds the man of sense,
While want of feeling is the fool's defence;
Arm'd with insensibility he comes,
When more repell'd, he but the more assumes,
And thus succeeds where fails the man of wit;
For where we cannot conquer we submit.

But come, my love! let us examine now
These Charges all;—say, what shall we avow,
Admit, deny; and which defend and how?
That old affair between your friend and you,
When your fond Sailor bade his home adieu,
May be forgotten; yet we should prepare
For all events: and are you guarded there?

C. Oh! 't is long since—I might the whole deny—
'So poor and so contemptible a lie!
'Charles, if 't is pleasant to abuse your friend,
'Let there be something that she may defend;
'This is too silly—'

          D. Well you may appear
With so much spirit—not a witness near;
Time puzzles judgment, and, when none explain,
You may assume the airs of high disdain.

But for my Brother: night and morn were you
Together found, th' inseparable two,
Far from the haunts of vulgar prying men—
In the old abbey—in the lonely glen—
In the beech-wood—within the quarry made
By hands long dead—within the silent glade,
Where the moon gleams upon the spring that flows
By the grey willows as they stand in rows—
Shall I proceed? there 's not a quiet spot
In all the parish where the pair were not,
Oft watch'd, oft seen. You must not so despise
This weighty charge—Now, what will you devise?

    C. 'Her brother! What, sir? jealous of a child!
'A friend's relation! Why, the man is wild!
'A boy not yet at college! Come, this proves
'Some truth in you! This is a freak of Love's:
'I must forgive it, though I know not how
'A thing so very simple to allow.
'Pray, if I meet my cousin's little boy,
'And take a kiss, would that your peace annoy?
'But I remember Delia—yet to give
'A thought to this is folly, as I live—
'But I remember Delia made her prayer
'That I would try and give the Boy an air;
'Yet awkward he, for all the pains we took—
'A bookish boy, his pleasure is his book;
'And since the lad is grown to man's estate,
'We never speak—your bookish youth I hate.'

    D. Right! and he cannot tell, with all his art,
Our father's will compell'd you both to part.

    C. Nay, this is needless—

D. Oh! when you are tried,
And taught for trial, must I feed your pride?
Oh! that's the vice of which I still complain:
Men could not triumph were not women vain.
But now proceed—say *boyhood* in this case
(The last obscure one) shields you from disgrace.
But what of Shelley? all your foes can prove,
And all your friends, that here indeed was love.
For three long months you met as lovers meet,
And half the town has seen him at your feet;
Then, on the evil day that saw you part,
Your ashy looks betray'd your aching heart.
With this against you——

      C. This, my watchful friend,
Confess I cannot; therefore must defend.

  'Shelley! dear Charles, how enter'd he your mind?
'Well may they say that jealousy is blind!
'Of all the men who talk'd with me of love,
'His were the offers I could least approve;
'My father's choice—and, Charles, you must agree
'That my good father seldom thinks with me—
'Or his had been the grief, while thou wert toss'd at sea!
'It was so odious—when that man was near,
'My father never could himself appear;
'Had I received his fav'rite with a frown,
'Upon my word he would have knock'd me down.'

  D. Well! grant you durst not frown—but people say
That you were dying when he went away:——
Yes! you were ill! of that no doubts remain;
And how explain it?——

C. Oh! I 'll soon explain:—

    'I sicken'd, say you, when the man was gone?
'Could I be well, if sickness would come on?
'Fact follows fact: but is 't of Nature's laws
'That one of course must be the other's cause?
'Just as her husband tried his fav'rite gun,
'My cousin brought him forth his first-born son.
'The birth might either flash or fright succeed,
'But neither, sure, were causes of the deed.
'That Shelley left us, it is very true—
'That sickness found me, I confess it too;
'But that the one was cause, and one effect,
'Is a conceit I utterly reject.
'You may, my Friend, demonstrate, if you please,
'That disappointment will bring on disease;
'But, if it should, I would be glad to know
'If 't is a quinsy that such griefs bestow?
'A heart may suffer, if a lady dote;
'But will she feel her anguish in the throat?
'I 've heard of pangs that tender folks endure,
'But not that linctuses and blisters cure.'

    Your thoughts, my Delia?—

                D. What I think of this?
Why! if he smile, it is not much amiss:
But there are humours; and, by them possess'd,
A lover will not hearken to a jest.

    Well, let this pass!—but, for the next affair:
We know your father was indignant there;
He hated Miller. Say! if Charles should press
For explanation, what would you confess?

Your cannot there on his commands presume;
Besides, you fainted in a public room;
There own'd your flame, and, like heroic maid,
The sovereign impulse of your will obey'd.
What, to your thinking, was the world's disdain?
You could retort its insolence again:
Your boundless passion boldly you avow'd,
And spoke the purpose of your soul aloud:
Associates, servants, friends, alike can prove
The world-defying force of Celia's love.
Did she not wish, nay vow, to poison her
Whom, some durst whisper, Damon could prefer?
And then that frantic quarrel at the ball—
It must be known, and he will hear it all.
Nay! never frown, but cast about, in time,
How best to answer what he thinks a crime:
For what he thinks might have but little weight,
If you could answer—

   C. Then I 'll answer straight—
Not without Truth; for who would vainly tell
A wretched lie, when Truth might serve as well?
Had I not fever? Is not that the bane
Of human wisdom? Was I not insane?

 'Oh! Charles, no more! would you recall the day
'When it pleased Fate to take my wits away?
'How can I answer for a thousand things
'That this disorder to the sufferer brings?
'Is it not known, the men whom you dislike
'Are those who now the erring fancy strike?
'Nor would it much surprise me, if 't were true,
'That in those days of dread I slighted you:

'When the poor mind, illumined by no spark
'Of reason's light, was wandering in the dark,
'You must not wonder, if the vilest train
'Of evil thoughts were printed on the brain;
'Nor if the loyal and the faithful prove
'False to their king, and faithless to their love.'
Your thoughts on this?

          D. With some you may succeed
By such bold strokes; but they must love indeed.

  C. Doubt you his passion?—

           D. But, in five long years
The passion settles—then the reason clears:
Turbid is love, and to ferment inclined,
But by and by grows sober and refined,
And peers for facts; but if one can't rely
On truth, one takes one's chance—you can but try.

Yet once again I must attention ask
To a new Charge, and then resign my task.
I would not hurt you; but confess at least
That you were partial to that handsome Priest;
Say what they will of his religious mind,
He was warm-hearted, and to ladies kind;
Now, with his reverence you were daily seen,
When it was winter and the weather keen;
Traced to the mountains when the winds were strong,
And roughly bore you, arm in arm, along—
That wintry wind, inspired by love or zeal,
You were too faithful or too fond to feel.
Shielded from inward and from outward harm
By the strong spirit and the fleshly arm—

The winter-garden you could both admire,
And leave his sisters at the parlour fire;
You trusted not your speech these dames among—
Better the teeth should chatter than the tongue!
Did not your father stop the pure delight
Of this perambulating Love at night?
It is reported that his craft contrived
To get the Priest with expedition wived
And sent away; for fathers will suspect
Her inward worth, whose ways are incorrect.
Patience, my dear! your Lover *will* appear;
At this new tale, then, what will be your cheer?

'I hear', says he,—and he will look as grim
As if he heard his lass accusing him—
'I hear, my Celia, your alluring looks
'Kept the young Curate from his holy books;
'Parsons, we know, advise their flocks to pray;
'But 't is their duty—not the better they;
''T is done for policy, for praise, for pay:
'Or, let the very best be understood,
'They 're men, you know, and men are flesh and blood.
'Now, they do say—but let me not offend—
'You were too often with this pious friend,
'And spent your time'——

    C. 'As people ought to spend.
'And, sir, if you of some divine would ask
'Aid in your doubts, it were a happy task;
'But you—alas, the while!—are not perplex'd
'By the dark meaning of a threat'ning text;
'You rather censure her who spends her time
'In search of Truth, as if it were a crime!

'Could I your dread of vulgar scandal feel,
'To whom should I, in my distress, appeal?
'A time there may be, Charles, indeed there must,
'When you will need a faithful Priest to trust,
'In conscience tender, but in counsel just.
'Charles, for my Fame I would in prudence strive,
'And, if I could, would keep your Love alive;
'But there are things that our attention claim,
'More near than Love, and more desired than Fame!'

    D. 'But why in secret?' he will ask you—

                             C. 'Why?
'Oh! Charles, could you the doubting spirit spy,
'Had you such fears, all hearers you would shun;
'What one confesses should be heard by one.
'Your mind is gross, and you have dwelt so long
'With such companions, that you will be wrong:
'We fill our minds from those with whom we live,
'And as your fears are Nature's, I forgive;
'But learn your peace and my good name to prize,
'And fears of fancy let us both despise.'

    D. Enough, my friend! Now let the man advance—
You are prepared, and nothing leave to chance:
'T is not sufficient that we 're pure and just;
The wise to nothing but their wisdom trust.

    Will he himself appear, or will he send,
Duteous as warm! and not alarm my friend?

    We need not ask—behold! his servant comes:
His father's livery! no fond heart presumes:
Thus he prepares you—kindly gives you space
To arm your mind and rectify your face.

Now, read your letter—while my faithful heart
Feels all that his can dictate or impart.

Nay! bless you, love! what melancholy tale
Conveys that paper? Why so deadly pale?
It is his sister's writing, but the seal
Is red: he lives. What is it that you feel?

C. O! my dear friend! let us from man retreat,
Or never trust him if we chance to meet—
The fickle wretch! that from our presence flies
To any flirt that any place supplies,
And laughs at vows!—but see the Letter!—here—
'*Married at Guernsey!!!*'—Oh! the Villain, dear!

TALES OF THE HALL

BOOK I

THE HALL

*　　　*　　　*

IT was an ancient, venerable Hall,
And once surrounded by a moat and wall;
A part was added by a squire of taste,
Who, while unvalued acres ran to waste,
Made spacious rooms, whence he could look about
And mark improvements as they rose without:
He fill'd the moat, he took the wall away,
He thinn'd the park, and bade the view be gay:
The scene was rich, but he who should behold
Its worth was poor, and so the whole was sold.

*　　　*　　　*

* * *

Such was the man who from the world return'd,
Nor friend nor foe; he prized it not, nor spurn'd;
But came and sat him in his village down,
Safe from its smile, and careless of its frown:
He, fairly looking into life's account,
Saw frowns and favours were of like amount;
And viewing all—his perils, prospects, purse,
He said, 'Content! 't is well it is no worse'.

* * *

BOOK II

THE BROTHERS

REMARRIAGE

* * *

His father early lost, his mother tried
To live without him, liked it not, and—sigh'd
When for her widow'd hand an amorous youth
    applied:
She still was young, and felt that she could share
A lover's passion, and a husband's care;
Yet pass'd twelve years before her son was told,
To his surprise, 'Your father you behold'.

* * *

His mother chose, nor I the choice upbraid,
An Irish soldier of a house decay'd,
And passing poor, but precious in her eyes
As she in his; they both obtain'd a prize.

To do the captain justice, she might share
What of her jointure his affairs could spare:
Irish he was in his profusion—true,
But he was Irish in affection too;
And though he spent her wealth and made her grieve,
He always said 'My dear', and 'With your leave'.
Him she survived: she saw his boy possess'd
Of manly spirit, and then sank to rest.

*　　　　*　　　　*

THE SCHOOLMASTER

From him a smile was like the Greenland sun,
Surprising, nay portentous, when it shone.

*　　　　*　　　　*

BOOK III

BOYS AT SCHOOL
MORAL CRITICISM

*　　　　*　　　　*

'In judging others we can see too well
'Their grievous fall, but not how grieved they fell;
'Judging ourselves, we to our minds recall,
'Not how we fell, but how we grieved to fall.'

*　　　　*　　　　*

133

BOOK IV

ADVENTURES OF RICHARD

AUTUMN

*   *   *

It was a fair and mild autumnal sky,
And earth's ripe treasures met th' admiring eye,
As a rich beauty, when her bloom is lost,
Appears with more magnificence and cost:
The wet and heavy grass, where feet had stray'd,
Not yet erect, the wanderer's way betray'd;
Showers of the night had swell'd the deep'ning rill,
The morning breeze had urged the quick'ning mill;
Assembled rooks had wing'd their seaward flight,
By the same passage to return at night,
While proudly o'er them hung the steady kite,
Then turn'd him back, and left the noisy throng,
Nor deign'd to know them as he sail'd along.
Long yellow leaves, from oziers, strew'd around,
Choked the small stream, and hush'd the feeble sound.

*   *   *

DAYDREAMS

*   *   *

'Man takes his body to a country-seat,
'But minds, dear Richard, have their own retreat;
'Oft when the feet are pacing o'er the green
'The mind is gone where never grass was seen,
'And never thinks of hill, or vale, or plain,
'Till want of rest creates a sense of pain
'That calls that wandering mind, and brings it
      home again.'

*   *   *

*   *   *

'To me the wives of seamen loved to tell
'What storms endanger'd men esteem'd so well;
'What wond'rous things in foreign parts they saw,
'Lands without bounds, and people without law.
'No ships were wreck'd upon that fatal beach,
'But I could give the luckless tale of each;
'Eager I look'd till I beheld a face
'Of one disposed to paint their dismal case;
'Who gave the sad survivors' doleful tale,
'From the first brushing of the mighty gale
'Until they struck; and, suffering in their fate,
'I long'd the more they should its horrors state;
'While some, the fond of pity, would enjoy
'The earnest sorrows of the feeling boy.

'I sought the men return'd from regions cold,
'The frozen straits, where icy mountains roll'd;
'Some I could win to tell me serious tales
'Of boats uplifted by enormous whales,
'Or, when harpoon'd, how swiftly through the sea
'The wounded monsters with the cordage flee;
'Yet some uneasy thoughts assail'd me then,
'The monsters warr'd not with nor wounded men:
'The smaller fry we take, with scales and fins,
'Who gasp and die—this adds not to our sins;
'But so much blood! warm life, and frames so large
'To strike, to murder!—seem'd a heavy charge.

'They told of days where many goes to one—
'Such days as ours; and how a larger sun,

135

'Red, but not flaming, roll'd, with motion slow,
'On the world's edge, but never dropp'd below.
'There were fond girls who took me to their side
'To tell the story how their lovers died;
'They praised my tender heart, and bade me prove
'Both kind and constant when I came to love.
'In fact I lived for many an idle year
'In fond pursuit of agitations dear;
'For ever seeking, ever pleased to find,
'The food I loved, I thought not of its kind;
'It gave affliction while it brought delight,
'And joy and anguish could at once excite.'

*　　　*　　　*

'The open shops of craftsmen caught my eye,
'And there my questions met the kind reply:
'Men, when alone, will teach; but, in a crowd,
'The child is silent, or the man is proud;
'But, by themselves, there is attention paid
'To a mild boy, so forward, yet afraid.

'I made me interest at the inn's fire-side,
'Amid the scenes to bolder boys denied;
'For I had patrons there, and I was one,
'They judged, who noticed nothing that was done.
'"A quiet lad!" would my protector say;
'"To him, now, this is better than his play;
'"Boys are as men; some active, shrewd, and keen,
'"They look about if aught is to be seen;
'"And some, like Richard here, have not a mind
'"That takes a notice—but the lad is kind."

'I loved in summer on the heath to walk,
'And seek the shepherd—shepherds love to talk:
'His superstition was of ranker kind,
'And he with tales of wonder stored my mind—
'Wonders that he in many a lonely eve
'Had seen, himself, and therefore must believe.
'His boy, his Joe, he said, from duty ran,
'Took to the sea and grew a fearless man:
'"On yonder knoll—the sheep were in the fold—
'"His spirit pass'd me, shivering-like and cold!
'"I felt a fluttering, but I knew not how,
'"And heard him utter, like a whisper, 'Now!'
'"Soon came a letter from a friend—to tell
'"That he had fallen, and the time he fell".

*   *   *

'I loved to walk where none had walk'd before,
'About the rocks that ran along the shore;
'Or far beyond the sight of men to stray,
'And take my pleasure when I lost my way;
'For then 't was mine to trace the hilly heath,
'And all the mossy moor that lies beneath:
'Here had I favourite stations, where I stood
'And heard the murmurs of the ocean-flood,
'With not a sound beside except when flew
'Aloft the lapwing or the grey curlew,
'Who with wild notes my fancied power defied,
'And mock'd the dreams of solitary pride.

'I loved to stop at every creek and bay
'Made by the river in its winding way,
'And call to memory—not by marks they bare,
'But by the thoughts that were created there.

137

'Pleasant it was to view the sea-gulls strive
'Against the storm, or in the ocean dive,
'With eager scream, or when they dropping gave
'Their closing wings, to sail upon the wave;
'Then as the winds and waters raged around,
'And breaking billows mix'd their deafening sound,
'They on the rolling deep securely hung,
'And calmly rode the restless waves among.
'Nor pleased it less around me to behold,
'Far up the beach, the yesty sea-foam roll'd;
'Or, from the shore upborne, to see on high
'Its frothy flakes in wild confusion fly:
'While the salt spray that clashing billows form
'Gave to the taste a feeling of the storm.'

*   *   *

BOOK V

RUTH

*   *   *

'South in the port, and eastward in the street,
'Rose a small dwelling, my beloved retreat,
'Where lived a pair, then old; the sons had fled
'The home they fill'd: a part of them were dead;
'Married a part; while some at sea remain'd,
'And stillness in the seaman's mansion reign'd;
'Lord of some petty craft, by night and day
'The man had fish'd each fathom of the bay.

'My friend the matron woo'd me, quickly won,
'To fill the station of an absent son

138

'(Him whom at school I knew, and Peter known,
'I took his home and mother for my own):
'I read, and doubly was I paid to hear
'Events that fell upon no listless ear:
'She grieved to say her parents could neglect
'Her education!—'t was a sore defect;
'She, who had ever such a vast delight
'To learn, and now could neither read nor write:
'But hear she could, and from our stores I took,
'Librarian meet! at her desire, our book.

   'Full twenty volumes—I would not exceed
'The modest truth—were there for me to read;
'These a long shelf contain'd, and they were found
'Books truly speaking, volumes fairly bound:
'The rest—for some of other kinds remain'd,
'And these a board beneath the shelf contain'd—
'Had their deficiencies in part; they lack'd
'One side or both, or were no longer back'd;
'But now became degraded from their place,
'And were but pamphlets of a bulkier race.
'Yet had we pamphlets, an inviting store,
'From sixpence downwards—nay, a part were
          more;
'Learning abundance, and the various kinds
'For relaxation—food for different minds;
'A piece of Wingate—thanks for all we have—
'What we of figures needed, fully gave;
'Culpepper, new in numbers, cost but thrice
'The ancient volume's unassuming price,
'But told what planet o'er each herb had power,
'And how to take it in the lucky hour.

'History we had—wars, treasons, treaties, crimes,
'From Julius Cæsar to the present times;
'Questions and answers, teaching what to ask
'And what reply,—a kind, laborious task:
'A scholar's book it was, who, giving, swore
'It held the whole he wish'd to know, and more.
'And we had poets, hymns and songs divine;
'The most we read not, but allow'd them fine.

'Our tracts were many, on the boldest themes—
'We had our metaphysics, spirits, dreams,
'Visions and warnings, and portentous sights,
'Seen, though but dimly, in the doleful nights,
'When the good wife her wintry vigil keeps,
'And thinks alone of him at sea, and weeps.

'Add to all these our works in single sheets,
'That our Cassandras sing about the streets:
'These, as I read, the grave good man would say,
'"Nay, Hannah!" and she answer'd, "What is Nay?
'"What is there, pray, so hurtful in a song?
'"It is our fancy only makes it wrong;
'"His purer mind no evil thoughts alarm,
'"And innocence protects him like a charm".
'Then would the matron, when the song had pass'd,
'And her laugh over, ask a hymn at last;
'To the coarse jest she would attention lend,
'And to the pious psalm in reverence bend:
'She gave her every power and all her mind,
'As chance directed, or as taste inclined.

'More of our learning I will now omit;
'We had our Cyclopædias of Wit,
'And all our works—rare fate!—were to our genius fit.

'When I had read, and we were weary grown
'Of other minds, the dame disclosed her own:
'And long have I in pleasing terror stay'd
'To hear of boys trepann'd, and girls betray'd;
'Ashamed so long to stay, and yet to go afraid.
'I could perceive, though Hannah bore full well
'The ills of life, that few with her would dwell,
'But pass away, like shadows o'er the plain
'From flying clouds, and leave it fair again;
'Still every evil, be it great or small,
'Would one past sorrow to the mind recall,
'The grand disease of life, to which she turns,
'And common cares and lighter suffering spurns.
'"O! these are nothing,—they will never heed
'"Such idle contests, who have fought indeed,
'"And have the wounds unclosed."—I understood
'My hint to speak, and my design pursued,
'Curious the secret of that heart to find,
'To mirth, to song, to laughter loud inclined,
'And yet to bear and feel a weight of grief behind:
'How does she thus her little sunshine throw
'Always before her?—I should like to know.
'My friend perceived, and would no longer hide
'The bosom's sorrow.—Could she not confide
'In one who wept, unhurt—in one who felt, untried?

'"Dear child, I show you sins and sufferings strange,
'"But you, like Adam, must for knowledge change
'"That blissful ignorance: remember, then,
'"What now you feel should be a check on men;
'"For then your passions no debate allow,
'"And therefore lay up resolution now.

141

"'"'T is not enough, that, when you can persuade
"'"A maid to love, you know there 's promise made;
"'"'T is not enough that you design to keep
"'"That promise made, nor leave your lass to weep:
"'"But you must guard yourself against the sin,
"'"And think it such to draw the party in:
"'"Nay, the more weak and easy to be won,
"'"The viler you who have the mischief done.

"'"I am not angry, love; but men should know
"'"They cannot always pay the debt they owe
"'"Their plighted honour; they may cause the ill
"'"They cannot lessen, though they feel a will;
"'"For *he* had truth with love, but love in youth
"'"Does wrong, that cannot be repair'd by truth.

"'"*Ruth*—I may tell, too oft had she been told—
"'"Was tall and fair, and comely to behold,
"'"Gentle and simple, in her native place
"'"Not one compared with her in form or face;
"'"She was not merry, but she gave our hearth
"'"A cheerful spirit that was more than mirth.

"'"There was a sailor boy, and people said
"'"He was, as man, a likeness of the maid;
"'"But not in this—for he was ever glad,
"'"While Ruth was apprehensive, mild, and sad;
"'"A quiet spirit hers, and peace would seek
"'"In meditation: tender, mild, and meek!
"'"Her loved the lad most truly; and, in truth,
"'"She took an early liking to the youth:
"'"To her alone were his attentions paid,
"'"And they became the bachelor and maid.

142

'"He wish'd to marry, but so prudent we
'"And worldly wise, we said it could not be:
'"They took the counsel,—may be, they approved,—
'"But still they grieved and waited, hoped and loved.

'"Now, my young friend, when of such state I speak
'"As one of danger, you will be to seek;
'"You know not, Richard, where the danger lies
'"In loving hearts, kind words, and speaking eyes;
'"For lovers speak their wishes with their looks
'"As plainly, love, as you can read your books.
'"Then, too, the meetings and the partings, all
'"The playful quarrels in which lovers fall,
'"Serve to one end—each lover is a child,
'"Quick to resent and to be reconciled;
'"And then their peace brings kindness that remains,
'"And so the lover from the quarrel gains:
'"When he has fault that she reproves, his fear
'"And grief assure her she was too severe,
'"And that brings kindness; when he bears an ill,
'"Or disappointment, and is calm and still,
'"She feels his own obedient to her will,
'"And that brings kindness—and what kindness brings
'"I cannot tell you:—these were trying things.
'"They were as children, and they fell at length;
'"The trial, doubtless, is beyond their strength
'"Whom grace supports not; and will grace support
'"The too confiding, who their danger court?
'"Then they would marry, but were now too late;
'"All could their fault in sport or malice state;
'"And though the day was fix'd and now drew on,
'"I could perceive my daughter's peace was gone;

143

"'She could not bear the bold and laughing eye
"'That gazed on her,—reproach she could not fly;
"'Her grief she would not show, her shame could
          not deny:
"'For some with many virtues come to shame,
"'And some that lose them all preserve their name.

"'Fix'd was the day; but ere that day appear'd,
"'A frightful rumour through the place was heard;
"'War, who had slept a while, awaked once more,
"'And gangs came pressing till they swept the shore:
"'Our youth was seized and quickly sent away,
"'Nor would the wretches for his marriage stay,
"'But bore him off, in barbarous triumph bore,
"'And left us all our miseries to deplore:
"'There were wives, maids, and mothers on the beach,
"'And some sad story appertain'd to each;
"'Most sad to Ruth—to neither could she go!
"'But sat apart, and suffer'd matchless woe!
"'On the vile ship they turn'd their earnest view,
"'Not one last look allow'd,—not one adieu!
"'They saw the men on deck, but none distinctly knew.
"'And there she stay'd, regardless of each eye,
"'With but one hope—a fervent hope to die:
"'Nor cared she now for kindness—all beheld
"'Her, who invited none, and none repell'd;
"'For there are griefs, my child, that sufferers hide,
"'And there are griefs that men display with pride;
"'But there are other griefs that, so we feel,
"'We care not to display them nor conceal:
"'Such were our sorrows on that fatal day,
"'More than our lives the spoilers tore away;

'"Nor did we heed their insult—some distress
'"No form or manner can make more or less,
'"And this is of that kind—this misery of a Press!
'"They say such things must be—perhaps they must;
'"But, sure, they need not fright us and disgust;
'"They need not soul-less crews of ruffians send
'"At once the ties of humble love to rend:
'"A single day had Thomas stay'd on shore,
'"He might have wedded, and we ask'd no more;
'"And that stern man, who forced the lad away,
'"Might have attended, and have graced the day;
'"His pride and honour might have been at rest,
'"It is no stain to make a couple bless'd!
'"Bless'd!—no, alas! it was to ease the heart
'"Of one sore pang, and then to weep and part!
'"But this he would not.—English seamen fight
'"For England's gain and glory—it is right:
'"But will that public spirit be so strong,
'"Fill'd, as it must be, with their private wrong?
'"Forbid it, honour! one in all the fleet
'"Should hide in war, or from the foe retreat;
'"But is it just, that he who so defends
'"His country's cause should hide him from her
        friends?
'"Sure, if they must upon our children seize,
'"They might prevent such injuries as these;
'"Might hours—nay, days—in many a case allow,
'"And soften all the griefs we suffer now.
'"Some laws, some orders, might in part redress
'"The licensed insults of a British Press,
'"That keeps the honest and the brave in awe,
'"Where might is right, and violence is law.

"'Be not alarm'd, my child; there's none regard
"'What you and I conceive so cruel-hard:
"'There is compassion, I believe; but still
"'One wants the power to help, and one the will,
"'And so from war to war the wrongs remain,
"'While Reason pleads, and Misery sighs in vain.

"'Thus my poor Ruth was wretched and undone,
"'Nor had a husband for her only son,
"'Nor had he father; hope she did a while,
"'And would not weep, although she could not smile;
"'Till news was brought us that the youth was slain,
"'And then, I think, she never smiled again;
"'Or, if she did, it was but to express
"'A feeling far, indeed, from happiness!
"'Something that her bewilder'd mind conceived:
"'When she inform'd us that she never grieved,
"'But was right merry, then her head was wild,
"'And grief had gain'd possession of my child:
"'Yet, though bewilder'd for a time, and prone
"'To ramble much and speak aloud, alone,
"'Yet did she all that duty ever ask'd,
"'And more, her will self-govern'd and untask'd;
"'With meekness bearing all reproach, all joy
"'To her was lost; she wept upon her boy,
"'Wish'd for his death, in fear that he might live
"'New sorrow to a burden'd heart to give.

"'There was a Teacher, where my husband went—
"'*Sent*, as he told the people—what he meant
"'You cannot understand, but—he was sent:
"'This man from meeting came, and strove to win
"'Her mind to peace by drawing off the sin,

"'Or what it was, that, working in her breast,
"'Robb'd it of comfort, confidence, and rest:
"'He came and reason'd, and she seem'd to feel
"'The pains he took—her griefs began to heal;
"'She ever answer'd kindly when he spoke,
"'And always thank'd him for the pains he took;
"'So, after three long years, and all the while
"'Wrapp'd up in grief, she bless'd us with a smile,
"'And spoke in comfort; but she mix'd no more
"'With younger persons, as she did before.

"'Still Ruth was pretty; in her person neat;
"'So thought the Teacher, when they chanced to
        meet:
"'He was a weaver by his worldly trade,
"'But powerful work in the assemblies made;
"'People came leagues to town to hear him sift
"'The holy text,—he had the grace and gift;
"'Widows and maidens flock'd to hear his voice;
"'Of either kind he might have had his choice;—
"'But he had chosen—we had seen how shy
"'The girl was getting, my good man and I,—
"'That when the weaver came, she kept with us,
"'Where he his points and doctrines might discuss;
"'But in our bit of garden, or the room
"'We call our parlour, there he must not come:
"'She loved him not, and though she could attend
"'To his discourses, as her guide and friend,
"'Yet now to these she gave a listless ear,
"'As if a friend she would no longer hear;
"'This might he take for woman's art, and cried,
"''Spouse of my heart, I must not be denied!'—

"'Fearless he spoke, and I had hope to see
"'My girl a wife—but this was not to be.

    "'My husband, thinking of his worldly store,
"'And not, frail man, enduring to be poor,
"'Seeing his friend would for his child provide
"'And hers, he grieved to have the man denied:
"'For Ruth, when press'd, rejected him, and grew
"'To her old sorrow, as if that were new.
"''Who shall support her?' said her father, 'how
"'Can I, infirm and weak as I am now?
"'And here a loving fool'——This gave her pain,
"'Severe, indeed, but she would not complain:
"'Nor would consent, although the weaver grew
"'More fond, and would the frighten'd girl pursue.

    "'Oh! much she begg'd him to forbear, to stand
"'Her soul's kind friend, and not to ask her hand;
"'She could not love him.—'Love me!' he replied.—-
"''The love you mean is love unsanctified,
"'An earthly, wicked, sensual, sinful kind,
"'A creature-love, the passion of the blind.'
"'He did not court her, he would have her know,
"'For that poor love that will on beauty grow;
"'No! he would take her as the Prophet took
"'One of the harlots in the holy book;
"'And he look'd so ugly and severe!
"'And yet so fond—she could not hide her fear.

    "'This fondness grew her torment; she would fly,
"'In woman's terror, if he came but nigh;
"'Nor could I wonder he should odious prove,
"'So like a ghost that left a grave for love.

'"But still her father lent his cruel aid
'"To the man's hope, and she was more afraid;
'"He said no more she should his table share,
'"But be the parish or the Teacher's care.
'"'Three days I give you: see that all be right
'"On Monday morning—this is Thursday night—
'"Fulfil my wishes, girl! or else forsake my sight!'

'"I see her now; and, she that was so meek,
'"It was a chance that she had power to speak,
'"Now spoke in earnest—'Father! I obey,
'"And will remember the appointed day!'

'"Then came the man: she talk'd with him apart,
'"And, I believe, laid open all her heart;
'"But all in vain—she said to me, in tears,
'"'Mother! that man is not what he appears:
'"He talks of heaven, and let him, if he will,
'"But he has earthly purpose to fulfil;
'"Upon my knees I begg'd him to resign
'"The hand he asks: he said—It shall be mine:
'"What! did the holy men of Scripture deign
'"To hear a woman when she said Refrain?
'"Of whom they chose they took them wives,
            and these
'"Made it their study and their wish to please;
'"The women then were faithful and afraid;
'"As Sarah Abraham, they their lords obey'd,
'"And so she styled him; 't is in later days
'"Of foolish love that we our women praise,
'"Fall on the knee, and raise the suppliant hand,
'"And court the favour that we might command.—

149

""'O! my dear mother, when this man has power,
'"How will he treat me:—first may beasts devour!
'"Or death in every form that I could prove,
'"Except this selfish being's hateful love.'

'"I gently blamed her, for I knew how hard
'"It is to force affection and regard.

'"Ah! my dear lad, I talk to you as one
'"Who know the misery of a heart undone:
'"You know it not; but, dearest boy, when man,
'"Do not an ill because you find you can:
'"Where is the triumph? when such things men seek,
'"They only drive to wickedness the weak.

'"Weak was poor Ruth, and this good man so hard,
'"That to her weakness he had no regard:
'"But we had two days' peace; he came, and then
'"My daughter whisper'd, 'Would there were no men!
'"None to admire or scorn us, none to vex
'"A simple, trusting, fond, believing sex;
'"Who truly love the worth that men profess,
'"And think too kindly for their happiness."'

'Poor Ruth! few heroines in the tragic page
'Felt more than thee in thy contracted stage;
'Fair, fond, and virtuous, they our pity move,
'Impell'd by duty, agonized by love:
'But no Mandane, who in dread has knelt
'On the bare boards, has greater terrors felt,
'Nor been by warring passions more subdued,
'Than thou, by this man's grovelling wish pursued;
'Doom'd to a parent's judgment, all unjust,

'Doom'd the chance mercy of the world to trust,
'Or to wed grossness and conceal disgust.

'"If Ruth was frail, she had a mind too nice
'"To wed with that which she beheld as vice—
'"To take a reptile, who, beneath a show
'"Of peevish zeal, let carnal wishes grow:
'"Proud and yet mean, forbidding and yet full
'"Of eager appetites, devout and dull,
'"Waiting a legal right that he might seize
'"His own, and his impatient spirit ease,
'"Who would at once his pride and love indulge,
'"His temper humour, and his spite divulge.
'"This the poor victim saw—'A second time',
'"Sighing, she said, 'shall I commit the crime,
'"And now untempted? Can the form or rite
'"Make me a wife in my Creator's sight?
'"Can I the words without a meaning say?
'"Can I pronounce love, honour, or obey?
'"And if I cannot, shall I dare to wed,
'"And go a harlot to a loathed bed?
'"Never, dear mother! my poor boy and I
'"Will at the mercy of a parish lie;
'"Reproved for wants that vices would remove,
'"Reproach'd for vice that I could never love,
'"Mix'd with a crew long wedded to disgrace,
'"A vulgar, forward, equalizing race,—
'"And am I doom'd to beg a dwelling in that place?'

'"Such was her reasoning: many times she weigh'd
'"The evils all, and was of each afraid;
'"She loath'd the common board, the vulgar seat,
'"Where shame, and want, and vice, and sorrow meet,

151

'"Where frailty finds allies, where guilt insures retreat.
'"But peace again is fled: the Teacher comes,
'"And new importance, haughtier air assumes.

'"No hapless victim of a tyrant's love
'"More keenly felt, or more resisting strove
'"Against her fate: she look'd on every side,
'"But there were none to help her, none to guide;—
'"And he, the man who should have taught the soul,
'"Wish'd but the body in his base control.

'"She left her infant on the Sunday morn,
'"A creature doom'd to shame! in sorrow born;
'"A thing that languish'd, nor arrived at age
'"When the man's thoughts with sin and pain engage—
'"She came not home to share our humble meal,
'"Her father thinking what his child would feel
'"From his hard sentence—still she came not home.
'"The night grew dark, and yet she was not come;
'"The east-wind roar'd, the sea return'd the sound,
'"And the rain fell as if the world were drown'd:
'"There were no lights without, and my good man,
'"To kindness frighten'd, with a groan began
'"To talk of Ruth, and pray: and then he took
'"The Bible down, and read the holy book;
'"For he had learning: and when that was done
'"We sat in silence—Whither could we run?
'"We said; and then rush'd frighten'd from the door,
'"For we could bear our own conceit no more:
'"We call'd on neighbours—there she had not been;
'"We met some wanderers—ours they had not seen;
'"We hurried o'er the beach, both north and south,
'"Then join'd, and wander'd to our haven's mouth:

'"Where rush'd the falling waters wildly out,
'"I scarcely heard the good man's fearful shout,
'"Who saw a something on the billow ride,
'"And—'Heaven have mercy on our sins!' he cried,
'"'It is my child!'—and to the present hour
'"So he believes—and spirits have the power.

'"And she was gone! the waters wide and deep
'"Roll'd o'er her body as she lay asleep.
'"She heard no more the angry waves and wind,
'"She heard no more the threat'ning of mankind;
'"Wrapp'd in dark weeds, the refuse of the storm,
'"To the hard rock was borne her comely form!

'"But, oh! what storm was in that mind! what strife!
'"That could compel her to lay down her life!
'"For she was seen within the sea to wade,
'"By one at distance, when she first had pray'd;
'"Then to a rock within the hither shoal
'"Softly and with a fearful step she stole;
'"Then, when she gain'd it, on the top she stood
'"A moment still—and dropp'd into the flood!
'"The man cried loudly, but he cried in vain,—
'"She heard not then—she never heard again!
'"She had—pray, Heav'n!—she had that world in sight,
'"Where frailty mercy finds, and wrong has right;
'"But, sure, in this her portion such has been,
'"Well had it still remain'd a world unseen!'"

*   *   *

BOOK VI

ADVENTURES OF RICHARD, CONCLUDED

THE VICAR'S ENTOMOLOGY

*　　　　*　　　　*

'"And here again,—what call the learned this?
'"Both Hippobosca and Hirundinis?
'"Methinks the creature should be proud to find
'"That he employs the talents of mankind,
'"And that his sovereign master shrewdly looks,
'"Counts all his parts, and puts them in his books.
'"Well! go thy way, for I do feel it shame
'"To stay a being with so proud a name."'

*　　　　*　　　　*

LOVE'S TRIUMPH

*　　　　*　　　　*

'There is a college joy, to scholars known,
'When the first honours are proclaim'd their own;
'There is ambition's joy, when, in their race
'A man surpassing rivals gains his place:
'There is a beauty's joy amid a crowd
'To have that beauty her first fame allow'd;
'And there's the conqueror's joy, when, dubious held
'And long the fight, he sees the foe repell'd.

'But what are these, or what are other joys,
'That charm kings, conquerors, beauteous nymphs,
　　　and boys,
'Or greater yet, if greater yet be found,
'To that delight when love's dear hope is crown'd?

'To the first beating of a lover's heart,
'When the loved maid endeavours to impart,
'Frankly yet faintly, fondly yet in fear,
'The kind confession that he holds so dear?'

*   *   *

BOOK VII

THE ELDER BROTHER

LOVE AND GOUT

*   *   *

'Speak'st thou of her to whom thou mad'st thy vows,
'Of my fair sister, of thy lawful spouse?
'Or art thou talking some frail love about
'The rambling fit before th' abiding gout?'

'Nay, spare me, Brother, an adorer spare:
'Love and the gout! thou wouldst not these compare?'

'Yea and correctly; teasing ere they come,
'They then confine their victim to his home:
'In both are previous feints and false attacks,
'Both place the grieving patient on their racks;
'They both are ours, with all they bring, for life,
''T is not in us t' expel or gout or wife;
'On man a kind of dignity they shed,
'A sort of gloomy pomp about his bed:
'Then if he leaves them, go where'er he will,
'They have a claim upon his body still;
'Nay, when they quit him, as they sometimes do,
'What is there left t' enjoy or to pursue?'

*   *   *

155

*   *   *

'And when Distress has look'd us in the face,
'Has she not told him, "Thou art not Disgrace"?'

*   *   *

CONFESSION

*   *   *

     'Hear then the tale I tell:
'Who tells what thou shalt hear, esteems his hearer
    well.'   *   *   *

THE BUSINESS UNCLE

*   *   *

'He, when inform'd how men of taste could write,
'Look'd on his ledger with supreme delight:
'Then would he laugh, and, with insulting joy,
'Tell me aloud, "That's poetry, my boy!
'"These are your golden numbers—them repeat;
'"The more you have, the more you'll find them sweet;
'"Their numbers move all hearts—no matter for their
    feet.
'"Sir, when a man composes in this style,
'"What is to him a critic's frown or smile?
'"What is the puppy's censure or applause
'"To the good man who on his banker draws,
'"Buys an estate, and writes upon the grounds,
'"'Pay to A. B. a hundred thousand pounds'?
'"Thus, my dear nephew, thus your talents prove;
'"Leave verse to poets, and the poor to love."

  'Some months I suffer'd thus, compell'd to sit
'And hear a wealthy kinsman aim at wit.'

*   *   *

BOOK X

THE OLD BACHELOR

LIFE

*　　　*　　　*

For O! my friends, if this were all indeed,
Could we believe that nothing would succeed?
If all were but this daily dose of life,
Without a care or comfort, child or wife;
These walks for health with nothing more in view,
This doing nothing, and with labour too;
This frequent asking when 't is time to dine,
This daily dozing o'er the news and wine;
This age's riddle, when each day appears
So very long, so very short the years:
If this were all—but let me not suppose—
What then were life? whose virtues, trials, woes,
Would sleep th' eternal sleep, and there the scene
　　　would close.

*　　　*　　　*

And hence arises ancient men's report,
That days are tedious, and yet years are short.

BOOK XI

THE MAID'S STORY

MATERNAL ADVICE

*　　　*　　　*

'Have not one friend,' my mother cried, 'not one;
'That bane of our romantic triflers shun;
'Suppose her true, can she afford you aid?
'Suppose her false, your purpose is betray'd;
'And then in dubious points, and matters nice,
'How can you profit by a child's advice?

'While you are writing on from post to post,
'Your hour is over, and a man is lost:
'Girls of their hearts are scribbling; their desires,
'And what the folly of the heart requires,
'Dupes to their dreams—but I the truth impart,
'You cannot, child, afford to have a heart;
'Think nothing of it; to yourself be true,
'And keep life's first great business in your view;—
'Take it, dear Martha, for a useful rule,
'She who is poor is ugly or a fool;
'Or, worse than either, has a bosom fill'd
'With soft emotions, and with raptures thrill'd.'

* * *

'Secrets with girls, like loaded guns with boys,
'Are never valued till they make a noise.

* * *

'Like pence in children's pockets secrets lie
'In female bosoms—they must burn or fly.'

* * *

Such were my mother's cares to mend my lot,
And such her pupil, they succeeded not.

WAITING-MAID'S PHILOSOPHY

* * *

Kind-hearted Biddy tried my griefs to heal:—
'This is a nothing to what others feel;
'Life has a thousand sorrows worse than this;
'A lover lost is not a fortune, miss!
'One goes, another comes, and which is best
'There is no telling—set your heart at rest'.

* * *

BOOK XIII

DELAY HAS DANGER

*   *   *

'But now my tale,—and let the moral say,
'When hope can sleep, there 's Danger in Delay.
'Not that for rashness, Richard, I would plead,
'For unadvised alliance: no, indeed:
'Think ere the contract—but, contracted, stand
'No more debating, take the ready hand:
'When hearts are willing, and when fears subside,
'Trust not to time, but let the knot be tied;
'For when a lover has no more to do,
'He thinks in leisure, what shall I pursue?
'And then who knows what objects come in view?
'For when, assured, the man has nought to keep
'His wishes warm and active, then they sleep:
'Hopes die with fears; and then a man must lose
'All the gay visions, and delicious views,
'Once his mind's wealth! He travels at his ease,
'Nor horrors now nor fairy-beauty sees:
'When the kind goddess gives the wish'd assent,
'No mortal business should the deed prevent;
'But the bless'd youth should legal sanction seek
'Ere yet th' assenting blush has fled the cheek.

'And—hear me, Richard,—man has reptile-pride
'That often rises when his fears subside;
'When, like a trader feeling rich, he now
'Neglects his former smile, his humble bow,
'And, conscious of his hoarded wealth, assumes
'New airs, nor thinks how odious he becomes.

159

'There is a wandering, wavering train of thought,
'That something seeks where nothing should be sought,
'And will a self-delighted spirit move
'To dare the danger of pernicious love.

————————

'First be it granted all was duly said
'By the fond youth to the believing maid;
'Let us suppose with many a sigh there came
'The declaration of the deathless flame;—
'And so her answer—"She was happy then,
'"Bless'd in herself, and did not think of men;
'"And with such comforts in her present state,
'"A wish to change it was to tempt her fate:
'"That she would not; but yet she would confess
'"With him she thought her hazard would be less;
'"Nay, more, she would esteem, she would regard
        express;
'"But to be brief—if he could wait and see
'"In a few years what his desires would be."'

Henry, for years, read months, then weeks, nor found
The lady thought his judgment was unsound;
'For months read weeks', she read it to his praise,
And had some thoughts of changing it to *days*.

And here a short excursion let me make,
A lover tried, I think, for lovers' sake;
And teach the meaning in a lady's mind
When you can none in her expressions find:
Words are design'd that meaning to convey,
But often *Yea* is hidden in a *Nay!*
And what the charmer wills, some gentle hints betray.

Then, too, when ladies mean to yield at length,
They match their reasons with the lover's strength,
And, kindly cautious, will no force employ
But such as he can baffle or destroy.

As when heroic lovers beauty woo'd,
And were by magic's mighty art withstood,
The kind historian, for the dame afraid,
Gave to the faithful knight the stronger aid.

A downright *No!* would make a man despair,
Or leave for kinder nymph the cruel fair;
But '*No!* because I 'm very happy now,
'Because I dread th' irrevocable vow,
'Because I fear papa will not approve,
'Because I love not—no, I cannot love;
'Because you men of Cupid make a jest,
'Because—in short, a single life is best'.
A *No!* when back'd by reasons of such force,
Invites approach, and will recede of course.

Ladies, like towns besieged, for honour's sake,
Will some defence, or its appearance, make;
On first-approach there's much resistance made,
And conscious weakness hides in bold parade;
With lofty looks, and threat'nings stern and proud,
'Come, if you dare', is said in language loud,
But if th' attack be made with care and skill,
'Come', says the yielding party, 'if you will'.
Then each the other's valiant acts approve,
And twine their laurels in a wreath of love.

We now retrace our tale, and forward go,—
Thus Henry rightly read Cecilia's *No!*

His prudent father, who had duly weigh'd
And well approved the fortune of the maid,
Not much resisted, just enough to show
He knew his power, and would his son should know.

'Harry, I will, while I your bargain make,
'That you a journey to our patron take:
'I know her guardian; care will not become
'A lad when courting; as you must be dumb,
'You may be absent; I for you will speak,
'And ask what you are not supposed to seek.'

Then came the parting hour, and what arise
When lovers part! expressive looks and eyes,
Tender and tearful, many a fond adieu,
And many a call the sorrow to renew;
Sighs such as lovers only can explain,
And words that they might undertake in vain.

Cecilia liked it not; she had, in truth,
No mind to part with her enamour'd youth:
But thought it foolish thus themselves to cheat,
And part for nothing but again to meet.

Now Henry's father was a man whose heart
Took with his interest a decided part;
He knew his lordship, and was known for acts
That I omit,—they were acknowledged facts;
An interest somewhere—I the place forget,
And the good deed—no matter—'t was a debt:
Thither must Henry, and in vain the maid
Express'd dissent—the father was obey'd.

But though the maid was by her fears assail'd,
Her reason rose against them, and prevail'd;

Fear saw him hunting, leaping, falling—led,
Maim'd and disfigured, groaning to his bed;
Saw him in perils, duels,—dying,—dead.
But Prudence answer'd, 'Is not every maid
'With equal cause for him she loves afraid?'
And from her guarded mind Cecilia threw
The groundless terrors that will love pursue.

She had no doubts, and her reliance strong
Upon the honour that she would not wrong:
Firm in herself, she doubted not the truth
Of him, the chosen, the selected youth;
Trust of herself a trust in him supplied,
And she believed him faithful, though untried:
On her he might depend, in him she would confide.
If some fond girl express'd a tender pain
Lest some fair rival should allure her swain,
To such she answer'd with a look severe,
'Can one you doubt be worthy of your fear?'

My lord was kind,—a month had pass'd away,
And Henry stay'd,—he sometimes named a day;
But still my lord was kind, and Henry still must stay:
His father's words to him were words of fate—
'Wait, 't is your duty; 't is my pleasure, wait!'

In all his walks, in hilly heath or wood,
Cecilia's form the pensive youth pursued;
In the grey morning, in the silent noon,
In the soft twilight, by the sober moon,
In those forsaken rooms, in that immense saloon;
And he, now fond of that seclusion grown,
There reads her letters, and there writes his own.

'Here none approach', said he, 'to interfere,
'But I can think of my Cecilia here!'

But there did come—and how it came to pass
Who shall explain?—a mild and blue-eyed lass;—
It was the work of accident, no doubt—
The cause unknown—we say, 'as things fall out';
The damsel enter'd there, in wandering round about:
At first she saw not Henry; and she ran,
As from a ghost, when she beheld a man.

She was esteem'd a beauty through the Hall,
And so admitted, with consent of all;
And like a treasure was her beauty kept
From every guest who in the mansion slept,
Whether as friends who join'd the noble pair,
Or those invited by the steward there.

She was the daughter of a priest, whose life
Was brief and sad: he lost a darling wife,
And Fanny then her father, who could save
But a small portion; but his all he gave,
With the fair orphan, to a sister's care,
And her good spouse: they were the ruling pair—
Steward and steward's lady—o'er a tribe,
Each under each, whom I shall not describe.

This grave old couple, childless and alone,
Would, by their care, for Fanny's loss atone:
She had been taught in schools of honest fame;
And to the Hall, as to a home, she came,
My lord assenting: yet, as meet and right,
Fanny was held from every hero's sight,

Who might in youthful error cast his eyes
On one so gentle as a lawful prize,
On border land, whom, as their right or prey,
A youth from either side might bear away.
Some handsome lover of th' inferior class
Might as a wife approve the lovely lass;
Or some invader from the class above,
Who, more presuming, would his passion prove
By asking less—love only for his love.

This much experienced aunt her fear express'd,
And dread of old and young, of host and guest.
'Go not, my Fanny, in their way,' she cried,
'It is not right that virtue should be tried;
'So, to be safe, be ever at my side.'
She was not ever at that side; but still
Observ'd her precepts, and obey'd her will.

But in the morning's dawn and evening's gloom
She could not lock the damsel in her room;
And Fanny thought, 'I will ascend these stairs
'To see the chapel,—there are none at prayers;
'None', she believed, 'had yet to dress return'd,
'By whom a timid girl might be discern'd':
In her slow motion, looking, as she glides,
On pictures, busts, and what she met besides,
And speaking softly to herself alone,
Or singing low in melancholy tone;
And thus she rambled through the still domain,
Room after room, again, and yet again.

But, to retrace our story, still we say,
To this saloon the maiden took her way;

Where she beheld our Youth, and frighten'd ran,
And so their friendship in her fear began.

But dare she thither once again advance,
And still suppose the man will think it chance?
Nay, yet again, and what has chance to do
With this?—I know not: doubtless Fanny knew.

Now, of the meeting of a modest maid
And sober youth why need we be afraid?
And when a girl's amusements are so few
As Fanny's were, what would you have her do?
Reserved herself, a decent youth to find,
And just be civil, sociable, and kind,
And look together at the setting sun,
Then at each other—what the evil done?

Then Fanny took my little lord to play,
And bade him not intrude on Henry's way:
'O, he intrudes not!' said the Youth, and grew
Fond of the child, and would amuse him too;
Would make such faces, and assume such looks—
He loved it better than his gayest books.

When man with man would an acquaintance seek,
He will his thoughts in chosen language speak;
And they converse on divers themes, to find
If they possess a corresponding mind;
But man with woman has foundation laid,
And built up friendship, ere a word is said:
'T is not with words that they their wishes tell,
But with a language answering quite as well;
And thus they find, when they begin t' explore
Their way by speech, they knew it all before.

166

And now it chanced again the pair, when dark,
Met in their way when wandering in the park;
Not in the common path, for so they might,
Without a wonder, wander day or night;
But, when in pathless ways their chance will bring
A musing pair, we do admire the thing.

The Youth in meeting read the damsel's face,
As if he meant her inmost thoughts to trace:
On which her colour changed, as if she meant
To give her aid, and help his kind intent.

Both smiled and parted, but they did not speak—
The smile implied, 'Do tell me what you seek':
They took their different ways with erring feet,
And meet again, surprised that they could meet;
Then must they speak—and something of the air
Is always ready—''T is extremely fair!'

'It was so pleasant!' Henry said, 'the beam
'Of that sweet light so brilliant on the stream;
'And chiefly yonder, where that old cascade
'Has for an age its simple music made;
'All so delightful, soothing, and serene!
'Do you not feel it? not enjoy the scene?
'Something it has that words will not express,
'But rather hide, and make th' enjoyment less:
''T is what our souls conceive, 't is what our hearts
      confess'.

Poor Fanny's heart at these same words confess'd
How well he painted, and how rightly guess'd;
And, while they stood admiring their retreat,
Henry found something like a mossy seat;

But Fanny sat not; no, she rather pray'd
That she might leave him, she was so afraid.

'Not, sir, of you; your goodness I can trust,
'But folks are so censorious and unjust,
'They make no difference, they pay no regard
'To our true meaning, which is very hard
'And very cruel; great the pain it cost
'To lose such pleasure, but it must be lost;
'Did people know how free from thought of il
'One's meaning is, their malice would be still.'

At this she wept; at least a glittering gem
Shone in each eye, and there was fire in them,
For, as they fell, the sparkles, at his feet,
He felt emotions very warm and sweet.
'A lovely creature! not more fair than good,
'By all admired, by some, it seems, pursued,
'Yet self-protected by her virtue's force
'And conscious truth—What evil in discourse
'With one so guarded, who is pleased to trust
'Herself with me, reliance strong and just?'

Our lover then believed he must not seem
Cold to the maid who gave him her esteem:
Not manly this; Cecilia had his heart,
But it was lawful with his time to part;
It would be wrong in her to take amiss
A virtuous friendship for a girl like this;
False or disloyal he would never prove,
But kindness here took nothing from his love:
Soldiers to serve a foreign prince are known,
When not on present duty to their own;

So, though our bosom's queen we still prefer,
We are not always on our knees to her.
'Cecilia present, witness yon fair moon,
'And yon bright orbs, that fate would change as soon
'As my devotion; but the absent sun
'Cheers us no longer when his course is run;
'And then those starry twinklers may obtain
'A little worship till he shines again.'

The father still commanded, 'Wait a while',
And the son answer'd in submissive style,
Grieved, but obedient; and obedience teased
His lady's spirit more than grieving pleased;
That he should grieve in absence was most fit,
But not that he to absence should submit;
And in her letters might be traced reproof,
Distant indeed, but visible enough;
This should the wandering of his heart have stay'd:
Alas! the wanderer was the vainer made.

The parties daily met, as by consent,
And yet it always seem'd by accident;
Till in the nymph the shepherd had been blind
If he had fail'd to see a manner kind,
With that expressive look that seem'd to say,
'You do not speak, and yet you see you may'.

O, yes, he saw, and he resolved to fly,
And blamed his heart, unwilling to comply:
He sometimes wonder'd how it came to pass
That he had all this freedom with the lass;
Reserved herself, with strict attention kept,
And care and vigilance that never slept:

'How is it thus that they a beauty trust
'With me, who feel the confidence is just?
'And they, too, feel it; yes, they may confide',—
He said in folly, and he smiled in pride.
'T is thus our secret passions work their way,
And the poor victims know not they obey.

Familiar now became the wandering pair,
And there was pride and joy in Fanny's air;
For though his silence did not please the maid,
She judged him only modest and afraid:
The gentle dames are ever pleased to find
Their lovers dreading they should prove unkind;
So, blind by hope, and pleased with prospects gay,
The generous beauty gave her heart away
Before he said, 'I love!'—alas! he dared not say.

Cecilia yet was mistress of his mind,
But oft he wish'd her, like his Fanny, kind;
Her fondness soothed him, for the man was vain,
And he perceived that he could give her pain:
Cecilia liked not to profess her love,
But Fanny ever was the yielding dove;
Tender and trusting, waiting for the word,
And then prepared to hail her bosom's lord.

Cecilia once her honest love avow'd,
To make him happy, not to make him proud:
But she would not, for every asking sigh,
Confess the flame that waked his vanity;
But this poor maiden, every day and hour,
Would by fresh kindness feed the growing power;
And he indulged—vain being!—in the joy,
That he alone could raise it, or destroy:

A present good, from which he dared not fly,
Cecilia absent, and his Fanny by.

O! vain desire of youth, that in the hour
Of strong temptation, when he feels the power,
And knows how daily his desires increase,
Yet will he wait, and sacrifice his peace,
Will trust to chance to free him from the snare,
Of which long since his conscience said, Beware;
Or look for strange deliverance from that ill,
That he might fly, could he command the will!
How can he freedom from the future seek,
Who feels already that he grows too weak?
And thus refuses to resist, till time
Removes the power, and makes the way for crime;
Yet thoughts he had, and he would think, 'Forego
'My dear Cecilia? not for kingdoms! No!
'But may I, ought I not the friend to be
'Of one who feels this fond regard for me?
'I wrong no creature by a kindness lent
'To one so gentle, mild, and innocent:
'And for that fair one whom I still adore,
'By feeling thus I think of her the more';
And not unlikely, for our thoughts will tend
To those whom we are conscious we offend.

Had Reason whisper'd, 'Has Cecilia leave
'Some gentle youth in friendship to receive,
'And be to him the friend that you appear
'To this soft girl?—Would not some jealous fear
'Proclaim your thoughts that he approach'd too near?'

But Henry, blinded still, presumed to write
Of one in whom Cecilia would delight:

A mild and modest girl, a gentle friend,
If, as he hoped, her kindness would descend—
But what he fear'd to lose or hoped to gain
By writing thus, he had been ask'd in vain.

It was his purpose, every morn he rose,
The dangerous friendship he had made to close:
It was his torment nightly, ere he slept,
To feel his prudent purpose was not kept.
True, he has wonder'd why the timid maid
Meets him so often, and is not afraid;
And why that female dragon, fierce and keen,
Has never in their private walks been seen:
And often he has thought, 'What can their silence
    mean?
'They can have no design, or plot, or plan,—
'In fact, I know not how the thing began;
''T is their dependence on my credit here,
'And fear not, nor, in fact, have cause to fear'.

But did that pair, who seem'd to think that all
Unwatch'd will wander and unguarded fall,—
Did they permit a youth and maid to meet
Both unreproved? were they so indiscreet?

This sometimes enter'd Henry's mind, and then,
'Who shall account for women or for men?'
He said; 'or who their secret thoughts explore?
'Why do I vex me? I will think no more'.

My lord of late had said, in manner kind,
'My good friend Harry, do not think us blind!'
Letters had pass'd, though he had nothing seen,
His careful father and my lord between;

But to what purpose was to him unknown—
It might be borough business, or their own.
Fanny, it seem'd, was now no more in dread;
If one approach'd, she neither fear'd nor fled:
He mused on this,—'But wherefore her alarm?
'She knows me better, and she dreads no harm'.

Something his father wrote that gave him pain:
'I know not, son, if you should yet remain;—
'Be cautious, Harry, favours to procure
'We strain a point, but we must first be sure:
'Love is a folly,—that, indeed, is true,—
'But something still is to our honour due,
'So I must leave the thing to my good lord and you'.

But from Cecilia came remonstrance strong:—
'You write too darkly, and you stay too long;
'We hear reports; and, Henry, mark me well,—
'I heed not every tale that triflers tell;—
'Be you no trifler; dare not to believe
'That I am one whom words and vows deceive:
'You know your heart, your hazard you will learn,
'And this your trial:—instantly return'.

'Unjust, injurious, jealous, cruel maid!
'Am I a slave, of haughty words afraid?
'Can she who thus commands expect to be obey'd?
'O! how unlike this dear assenting soul,
'Whose heart a man might at his will control!'

Uneasy, anxious, fill'd with self-reproof,
He now resolved to quit his patron's roof;
And then again his vacillating mind
To stay resolved, and that her pride should find:

Debating thus, his pen the lover took,
And chose the words of anger and rebuke.

Again, yet once again, the conscious pair
Met, and 'O speak!' was Fanny's silent prayer;
And, 'I must speak', said the embarrass'd youth;
'Must save my honour, must confess the truth:
'Then I must lose her; but, by slow degrees,
'She will regain her peace, and I my ease'.

Ah! foolish man: to virtue true, nor vice,
He buys distress, and self-esteem the price;
And what his gain?—a tender smile and sigh
From a fond girl to feed his vanity.
Thus, every day they lived, and every time
They met, increased his anguish and his crime.

Still in their meetings they were oft-times nigh
The darling theme, and then pass'd trembling by;
On those occasions Henry often tried
For the sad truth—and then his heart denied
The utterance due: thus daily he became
The prey of weakness, vanity, and shame.

But soon a day, that was their doubts to close,
On the fond maid and thoughtless youth arose.
Within the park, beside the bounding brook,
The social pair their usual ramble took;
And there the steward found them: they could trace
News in his look, and gladness in his face.

He was a man of riches, bluff and big,
With clean brown broadcloth, and with white cut wig
He bore a cane of price, with riband tied,
And a fat spaniel waddled at his side:

To every being whom he met he gave
His looks expressive; civil, gay, or grave,
But condescending all; and each declared
How much he govern'd, and how well he fared.

This great man bow'd, not humbly, but his bow
Appear'd familiar converse to allow:
The trembling Fanny, as he came in view,
Within the chestnut grove in fear withdrew;
While Henry wonder'd, not without a fear,
Of that which brought th' important man so near:
Doubt was dispers'd by—'My esteem'd young man!'
As he with condescending grace began—
'Though you with youthful frankness nobly trust
'Your Fanny's friends, and doubtless think them just,—
'Though you have not, with craving soul, applied
'To us, and ask'd the fortune of your bride,—
'Be it our care that you shall not lament
'That love has made you so improvident.

'An orphan maid——Your patience! you shall have
'Your time to speak, I now attention crave;—
'Fanny, dear girl! has in my spouse and me
'Friends of a kind we wish our friends to be,
'None of the poorest——nay, sir, no reply,
'You shall not need——and we are born to die;
'And one yet crawls on earth, of whom, I say
'That what he has he cannot take away,—
'Her mother's father, one who has a store
'Of this world's good, and always looks for more;
'But, next his money, loves the girl at heart,
'And she will have it when they come to part'.

'Sir', said the Youth, his terrors all awake,
'Hear me, I pray, I beg,—for mercy's sake!
'Sir, were the secrets of my soul confess'd,
'Would you admit the truths that I protest
'Are such——your pardon——'
                              'Pardon! good, my friend,
'I not alone will pardon, I commend:
'Think you that I have no remembrance left
'Of youthful love, and Cupid's cunning theft?
'How nymphs will listen when their swains persuade,
'How hearts are gain'd, and how exchange is made?
'Come, sir, your hand——'
                              'In mercy, hear me now!'—
'I cannot hear you, time will not allow:
'You know my station, what on me depends,
'For ever needed—but we part as friends;
'And here comes one who will the whole explain,
'My better self—and we shall meet again.'

      'Sir, I entreat——'
                        'Then be entreaty made
'To her, a woman, one you may persuade;
'A little teasing, but she will comply,
'And loves her niece too fondly to deny.'

      'O! he is mad, and miserable I!'
Exclaim'd the Youth; 'but let me now collect
'My scatter'd thoughts, I something must effect'.

      Hurrying she came—'Now, what has he confess'd,
'Ere I could come to set your heart at rest?
'What! he has grieved you! Yet he, too, approves
'The thing! but man will tease you, if he loves.

176

'But now for business: tell me, did you think
'That we should always at your meetings wink?
'Think you, you walk'd unseen? There are who bring
'To me all secrets—O, you wicked thing!
'Poor Fanny! now I think I see her blush,
'All red and rosy, when I beat the bush;
'And hide your secret, said I, if you dare!
'So out it came, like an affrighten'd hare.
'"Miss!" said I, gravely; and the trembling maid
'Pleased me at heart to see her so afraid;
'And then she wept;—now, do remember this,
'Never to chide her when she does amiss;
'For she is tender as the callow bird,
'And cannot bear to have her temper stirr'd;—
'"Fanny," I said, then whisper'd her the name,
'And caused such looks—Yes, yours are just the same;
'But hear my story—When your love was known
'For this our child—she is, in fact, our own—
'Then, first debating, we agreed at last
'To seek my Lord, and tell him what had pass'd'.

 'To tell the Earl?'
       'Yes, truly, and why not?
'And then together we contrived our plot.'

 'Eternal God!'
     'Nay, be not so surprised,—
'In all the matter we were well advised;
'We saw my Lord, and Lady Jane was there,
'And said to Johnson, "Johnson, take a chair";
'True, we are servants in a certain way,
'But in the higher places so are they;
'We are obey'd in ours, and they in theirs obey:

'So Johnson bow'd, for that was right and fit,
'And had no scruple with the Earl to sit;—
'Why look you so impatient while I tell
'What they debated?—you must like it well.

'"Let them go on", our gracious Earl began;
'"They will go off", said, joking, my good man:
'"Well!" said the Countess,—she's a lover's friend,—
'"What if they do? they make the speedier end".——
'But be you more composed, for that dear child
'Is with her joy and apprehension wild:
'O! we have watch'd you on from day to day,—
'"There go the lovers!" we were wont to say;—
'But why that look?'—
                            'Dear madam, I implore
'A single moment!'—
                            'I can give no more:
'Here are your letters—"That's a female pen",
'Said I to Fanny.—"'T is his sister's then",
'Replied the maid.—No! never must you stray;
'Or hide your wanderings, if you should, I pray:
'I know, at least I fear, the best may err,
'But keep the by-walks of your life from her.
'That youth should stray is nothing to be told,
'When they have sanction in the grave and old,
'Who have no call to wander and transgress,
'But very love of change and wantonness.

'I prattle idly, while your letters wait,
'And then my Lord has much that he would state,
'All good to you—do clear that clouded face,
'And with good looks your lucky lot embrace.

178

'Now, mind that none with her divide your heart,
'For she would die ere lose the smallest part;
'And I rejoice that all has gone so well,
'For who th' effect of Johnson's rage can tell?
'He had his fears when you began to meet,
'But I assured him there was no deceit:
'He is a man who kindness will requite,
'But, injured once, revenge is his delight;
'And he would spend the best of his estates
'To ruin, goods and body, them he hates;
'While he is kind enough when he approves
'A deed that's done, and serves the man he loves:
'Come, read your letters—I must now be gone,
'And think of matters that are coming on.'

Henry was lost,—his brain confused, his soul
Dismay'd and sunk, his thoughts beyond control;
Borne on by terror, he foreboding read
Cecilia's letter! and his courage fled:
All was a gloomy, dark, and dreadful view;
He felt him guilty, but indignant too;
And as he read, he felt the high disdain
Of injured men—'She may repent in vain'.

Cecilia much had heard, and told him all
That scandal taught—'A servant at the Hall,
'Or servant's daughter, in the kitchen bred,
'Whose father would not with her mother wed,
'Was now his choice! a blushing fool, the toy,
'Or the attempted, both of man and boy;
'More than suspected, but without the wit
'Or the allurements for such creatures fit;

'Not virtuous though unfeeling, cold as ice
'And yet not chaste, the weeping fool of vice;
'Yielding, not tender; feeble, not refined;
'Her form insipid, and without a mind.

'Rival! she spurn'd the word; but let him stay,
'Warn'd as he was! beyond the present day,
'Whate'er his patron might object to this,
'The uncle-butler, or the weeping miss—
'Let him from this one single day remain,
'And then return! he would, to her, in vain;
'There let him then abide, to earn or crave
'Food undeserved! and be with slaves a slave.'

Had reason guided anger, govern'd zeal,
Or chosen words to make a lover feel,
She might have saved him—anger and abuse
Will but defiance and revenge produce.

'Unjust and cruel, insolent and proud!'
He said, indignant, and he spoke aloud.
'Butler! and servant! Gentlest of thy sex,
'Thou wouldst not thus a man who loved thee vex;
'Thou wouldst not thus to vile report give ear,
'Nor thus enraged for fancied crimes appear:
'I know not what, dear maid!—if thy soft smiles
        were here.'

And then, that instant, there appear'd the maid,
By his sad looks in her approach dismay'd;
Such timid sweetness, and so wrong'd, did more
Than all her pleading tenderness before.
In that weak moment, when disdain and pride,
And fear and fondness, drew the man aside,—

In this weak moment, 'Wilt thou,' he began,
'Be mine?' and joy o'er all her features ran:
'I will!' she softly whisper'd; but the roar
Of cannon would not strike his spirit more;
E'en as his lips the lawless contract seal'd,
He felt that conscience lost her seven-fold shield,
And honour fled; but still he spoke of love,
And all was joy in the consenting dove.

That evening all in fond discourse was spent,
When the sad lover to his chamber went,
To think on what had pass'd, to grieve, and to repent:
Early he rose, and look'd with many a sigh
On the red light that fill'd the eastern sky:
Oft had he stood before, alert and gay,
To hail the glories of the new-born day;
But now dejected, languid, listless, low,
He saw the wind upon the water blow,
And the cold stream curl'd onward as the gale
From the pine-hill blew harshly down the dale;
On the right side the youth a wood survey'd,
With all its dark intensity of shade;
Where the rough wind alone was heard to move,
In this, the pause of nature and of love,
When now the young are rear'd, and when the old,
Lost to the tie, grow negligent and cold:
Far to the left he saw the huts of men,
Half hid in mist that hung upon the fen;
Before him swallows, gathering for the sea,
Took their short flights, and twitter'd on the lea;
And, near, the bean-sheaf stood, the harvest done,
And slowly blacken'd in the sickly sun;

All these were sad in nature, or they took
Sadness from him, the likeness of his look,
And of his mind—he ponder'd for a while,
Then met his Fanny with a borrow'd smile.

Not much remain'd; for money and my Lord
Soon made the father of the youth accord;
His prudence half resisted, half obey'd,
And scorn kept still the guardians of the maid:
Cecilia never on the subject spoke,
She seem'd as one who from a dream awoke;
So all was peace, and soon the married pair
Fix'd with fair fortune in a mansion fair.

Five years had pass'd, and what was Henry then?
The most repining of repenting men;
With a fond, teasing, anxious wife, afraid
Of all attention to another paid;
Yet powerless she her husband to amuse,
Lives but t' entreat, implore, resent, accuse;
Jealous and tender, conscious of defects,
She merits little, and yet much expects;
She looks for love that now she cannot see,
And sighs for joy that never more can be;
On his retirements her complaints intrude,
And fond reproof endears his solitude:
While he her weakness (once her kindness) sees,
And his affections in her languor freeze;
Regret, uncheck'd by hope, devours his mind,
He feels unhappy, and he grows unkind.

'Fool! to be taken by a rosy cheek,
'And eyes that cease to sparkle or to speak;

'Fool! for this child my freedom to resign,
'When one the glory of her sex was mine;
'While from this burden to my soul I hide,
'To think what Fate has dealt, and what denied.

  'What fiend possess'd me when I tamely gave
'My forced assent to be an idiot's slave?
'Her beauty vanish'd, what for me remains?
'Th' eternal clicking of the galling chains:
'Her person truly I may think my own,
'Seen without pleasure, without triumph shown:
'Doleful she sits, her children at her knees,
'And gives up all her feeble powers to please:
'Whom I, unmoved, or moved with scorn, behold.
'Melting as ice, as vapid and as cold.'

  Such was his fate, and he must yet endure
The self-contempt that no self-love can cure:
Some business call'd him to a wealthy town
When unprepared for more than Fortune's frown;
There at a house he gave his luckless name,
The master absent, and Cecilia came.
Unhappy man! he could not, dared not speak,
But look'd around, as if retreat to seek:
This she allow'd not; but, with brow severe,
Ask'd him his business, sternly bent to hear;
He had no courage, but he view'd that face
As if he sought for sympathy and grace;
As if some kind returning thought to trace:
In vain; not long he waited, but, with air
That of all grace compell'd him to despair,
She rang the bell, and, when a servant came,
Left the repentant traitor to his shame;

But, going, spoke, 'Attend this person out,
'And, if he speaks, hear what he comes about!'
Then, with cool curtsy, from the room withdrew,
That seem'd to say, 'Unhappy man, adieu!'

Thus will it be when man permits a vice
First to invade his heart, and then entice;
When wishes vain and undefined arise,
And that weak heart deceive, seduce, surprise;
When evil Fortune works on Folly's side,
And rash Resentment adds a spur to Pride;—
Then life's long troubles from those actions come,
In which a moment may decide our doom.

BOOK XIV

THE NATURAL DEATH OF LOVE

*   *   *

HENRY AND EMMA

E. Well, my good sir, I shall contend no more;
But, O! the vows you made, the oaths you swore!

H. To love you always:—I confess it true;
And do I not? If not, what can I do?
Moreover, think what you yourself profess'd,
And then the subject may for ever rest.

E. Yes, sir, obedience I profess'd; I know
My debt, and wish to pay you all I owe,
Pay without murmur; but that vow was made
To you who said it never should be paid.—

184

You may remember—it is not so long
Since you affirm'd that I could not be wrong;
I told you then—you recollect, I told
The very truth—that humour would not hold;
Not that I thought, or ever could suppose,
The mighty raptures were so soon to close—
Poetic flights of love all sunk in sullen prose.

Do you remember how you used to hang
Upon my looks? your transports when I sang?
I play'd—you melted into tears; I moved—
Voice, words, and motion, how you all approved;
A time when Emma reign'd, a time when Henry loved:
You recollect?

H.   Yes, surely; and then why
The needless truths? do I the facts deny?
For this remonstrance I can see no need,
Or this impatience—if you do, proceed.

E. O! that is now so cool, and with a smile
That sharpens insult—I detest the style;
And, now I talk of styles, with what delight
You read my lines—I then, it seems, could write;
In short, when I was present, you could see
But one dear object, and you lived for me;
And now, sir, what your pleasure? Let me dress,
Sing, speak, or write, and you your sense express
Of my poor taste—my words are not correct;
In all I do is failing or defect—
Some error you will seek, some blunder will detect;
And what can such dissatisfaction prove?
I tell you, Henry, you have ceased to love.

H. I own it not; but if a truth it be,
It is the fault of nature, not of me.
Remember you, my love, the fairy tale,
Where the young pairs were spell-bound in the vale?
When all around them gay or glorious seem'd,
And of bright views and ceaseless joys they dream'd?
Young love and infant life no more could give—
They said but half, when they exclaim'd, 'We live!'
All was so light, so lovely, so serene,
And not a trouble to be heard or seen;
Till, melting into truth, the vision fled,
And there came miry roads and thorny ways instead.

Such was our fate, my charmer! we were found
A wandering pair, by roguish Cupid bound;
All that I saw was gifted to inspire
Grand views of bliss, and wake intense desire
Of joys that never pall, of flights that never tire;
There was that purple light of love, that bloom,
That ardent passions in their growth assume,
That pure enjoyment of the soul—O! weak
Are words such loves and glowing thoughts to speak!
I sought to praise thee, and I felt disdain
Of my own effort; all attempts were vain.

Nor they alone were charming; by that light
All loved of thee grew lovely in my sight;
Sweet influence not its own in every place
Was found, and there was found in all things grace;
Thy shrubs and plants were seen new bloom to bear,
Not the Arabian sweets so fragrant were,
Nor Eden's self, if aught with Eden might compare.

186

You went the church-way walk, you reach'd the farm,
And gave the grass and babbling springs a charm;
Crop, whom you rode,—sad rider though you be,—
Thenceforth was more than Pegasus to me.
Have I not woo'd your snarling cur to bend
To me the paw and greeting of a friend?
And all his surly ugliness forgave,
Because, like me, he was my Emma's slave?
Think you, thus charm'd, I would the spell revoke?
Alas! my love, we married, and it broke!

Yet no deceit or falsehood stain'd my breast,
What I asserted might a saint attest;
Fair, dear, and good thou wert—nay, fairest, dearest, best:
Nor shame, nor guilt, nor falsehood I avow,
But 't is by heaven's own light I see thee now;
And if that light will all those glories chase,
'T is not my wish that will the good replace.

E. O! sir, this boyish tale is mighty well,
But 't was your falsehood that destroy'd the spell:
Speak not of nature, 't is an evil mind
That makes you to accustom'd beauties blind;
You seek the faults yourself, and then complain you find.

H. I sought them not: but, madam, 't is in vain
The course of love and nature to restrain.
Lo! when the buds expand, the leaves are green,
Then the first opening of the flower is seen;
Then comes the honey'd breath and rosy smile,
That with their sweets the willing sense beguile;
But, as we look, and love, and taste, and praise,
And the fruit grows, the charming flower decays;

Till all is gather'd, and the wintry blast
Moans o'er the place of love and pleasure past.

So 't is with beauty—such the opening grace
And dawn of glory in the youthful face;
Then are the charms unfolded to the sight,
Then all is loveliness and all delight;
The nuptial tie succeeds the genial hour,
And, lo! the falling off of beauty's flower;
So through all nature is the progress made,—
The bud, the bloom, the fruit,—and then we fade.

Then sigh no more,—we might as well retain
The year's gay prime as bid that love remain—
That fond, delusive, happy, transient spell,
That hides us from a world wherein we dwell,
And forms and fits us for that fairy ground
Where charming dreams and gay conceits abound;
Till comes at length th' awakening strife and care,
That we, as tried and toiling men, must share.

E. O! sir, I must not think that Heaven approves
Ungrateful man or unrequited loves;
Nor that we less are fitted for our parts
By having tender souls and feeling hearts.

H. Come, my dear friend, and let us not refuse
The good we have, by grief for that we lose;
But let us both the very truth confess;
This must relieve the ill, and may redress.

E. O! much I fear! I practised no deceit;
Such as I am I saw you at my feet:
If for a goddess you a girl would take,
'T is you yourself the disappointment make.

H. And I alone!—O! Emma, when I pray'd
For grace from thee, transported and afraid,
Now raised to rapture, now to terror doom'd,
Was not the goddess by the girl assumed?
Did not my Emma use her skill to hide—
Let us be frank—her weakness and her pride?
Did she not all her sex's arts pursue,
To bring the angel forward to my view?
Was not the rising anger oft suppress'd?
Was not the waking passion hush'd to rest?
And when so mildly sweet you look'd and spoke,
Did not the woman deign to wear a cloak?
A cloak she wore, or, though not clear my sight,
I might have seen her—think you not I might?

E. O! this is glorious!—while your passion lives,
To the loved maid a robe of grace it gives;
And then, unjust! beholds her with surprise,
Unrobed, ungracious, when the passion dies.

H. For this, my Emma, I to Heaven appeal,
I felt entirely what I seem'd to feel;
Thou wert all precious in my sight, to me
The being angels are supposed to be;
And am I now of my deception told,
Because I'm doom'd a woman to behold?

E. Sir! in few words, I would a question ask—
Mean these reproaches that I wore a mask?
Mean you that I by art or caution tried
To show a virtue, or a fault to hide?

H. I will obey you.—When you seem'd to feel
Those books we read, and praised them with such zeal,

Approving all that certain friends approved,
Was it the pages or the praise you loved?
Nay, do not frown—I much rejoiced to find
Such early judgment in such gentle mind;
But, since we married, have you deigned to look
On the grave subjects of one favourite book?
Or have the once applauded pages power
T' engage their warm approver for an hour?

Nay, hear me further.—When we view'd that dell
Where lie those ruins—you must know it well—
When that worn pediment your walk delay'd,
And the stream gushing through the arch decay'd—
When at the venerable pile you stood,
Till the does ventured on our solitude,
We were so still! before the growing day
Call'd us reluctant from our seat away—
Tell me, was all the feeling you express'd
The genuine feeling of my Emma's breast;
Or was it borrow'd, that her faithful slave
The higher notion of her taste might have?
So may I judge, for of that lovely scene
The married Emma has no witness been;
No more beheld that water, falling, flow
Through the green fern that there delights to grow.

Once more, permit me. Well, I know, you feel
For suffering men, and would their sufferings heal,
But when at certain huts you chose to call,
At certain seasons, was compassion all?
I there beheld thee, to the wretched dear
As angels to expiring saints appear

When whispering hope—I saw an infant press'd
And hush'd to slumber on my Emma's breast!
Hush'd be each rude suggestion!—Well I know
With a free hand your bounty you bestow;
And to these objects frequent comforts send,
But still they see not now their pitying friend.
A merchant, Emma, when his wealth he states,
Though rich, is faulty if he over-rates
His real store; and gaining greater trust
For the deception, should we deem him just?

If in your singleness of heart you hide
No flaw or frailty, when your truth is tried,
And time has drawn aside the veil of love,
We may be sorry, but we must approve;
The fancied charms no more our praise compel,
But doubly shines the worth that stands so well.

   E. O! precious are you all, and prizes too,
Or could we take such guilty pains for you?
Believe it not—As long as passion lasts,
A charm about the chosen maid it casts;
And the poor girl has little more to do
Than just to keep in sight as you pursue:
Chance to a ruin leads her; you behold,
And straight the angel of her taste is told:
Chance to a cottage leads you, and you trace
A virtuous pity in the angel's face;
She reads a work you chance to recommend,
And likes it well—at least she likes the friend;
But when it chances this no more is done,
She has not left one virtue—no! not one!

But be it said, good sir, we use such art,
Is it not done to hold a fickle heart,
And fix a roving eye? Is that design
Shameful or wicked that would keep you mine?
If I confess the art, I would proceed
To say of such that every maid has need.

Then when you flatter—in your language, praise—
In our own view you must our value raise;
And must we not, to this mistaken man,
Appear as like his picture as we can?
If you will call—nay, treat us as divine,
Must we not something to your thoughts incline?
If men of sense will worship whom they love,
Think you the idol will the error prove?
What! show him all her glory is pretence,
And make an idiot of this man of sense?

Then, too, suppose we should his praise refuse,
And clear his mind, we may our lover lose;
In fact, you make us more than nature makes,
And we, no doubt, consent to your mistakes;
You will, we know, until the frenzy cools,
Enjoy the transient paradise of fools;
But, fancy fled, you quit the blissful state,
And truth for ever bars the golden gate.

H. True! but how ill each other to upbraid,
'T is not our fault that we no longer stay'd;
No sudden fate our lingering love suppress'd,
It died an easy death, and calmly sank to rest;
To either sex is the delusion lent,
And when it fails us, we should rest content;
'T is cruel to reproach, when bootless to repent.

E. Then wise the lovers who consent to wait,
And, always lingering, never try the state;
But, hurried on by what they call their pain,
And I their bliss, no longer they refrain;
To ease that pain, to lose that bliss, they run
To the church magi, and the thing is done:
A spell is utter'd, and a ring applied,
And forth they walk a bridegroom and a bride,
To find this counter-charm, this marriage rite,
Has put their present fallacies to flight!
But tell me, Henry, should we truly strive,
May we not bid the happy dream revive?

H. Alas! they say when weakness or when vice
Expels a foolish pair from Paradise,
The guardian power to prayer has no regard,—
The knowledge once obtain'd, the gate is barr'd;
Or could we enter, we should still repine,
Unless we could the knowledge too resign.
Yet let us calmly view our present fate,
And make a humbler Eden of our state;
With this advantage, that what now we gain,
Experience gives and prudence will retain.

E. Ah! much I doubt—when you in fury broke
That lovely vase by one impassion'd stroke,
And thousand china fragments met my sight,
Till rising anger put my grief to flight;
As well might you the beauteous jar repiece,
As joy renew and bid vexation cease.

H. Why, then 't is wisdom, Emma, not to keep
These griefs in memory; they had better sleep.

There was a time when this heaven-guarded isle,
Whose valleys flourish—nay, whose mountains smile—
Was sterile, wild, deform'd, and beings rude
Creatures scarce wilder than themselves pursued;
The sea was heard around a waste to howl,
The night-wolf answer'd to the whooting owl,
And all was wretched:—Yet who now surveys
The land withholds his wonder and his praise?
Come, let us try and make our moral view
Improve like this—this have we power to do.

E. O! I'll be all forgetful, deaf and dumb,
And all you wish, to have these changes come.

H. And come they may, if not as heretofore,
We cannot all the lovely vase restore;
What we beheld in Love's perspective glass
Has pass'd away—one sigh! and let it pass:
It was a blissful vision, and it fled,
And we must get some actual good instead.

    *   *   *

Each on the other must in all depend,
The kind adviser, the unfailing friend;
Through the rough world we must each other aid,
Leading and led, obeying and obey'd.

    *   *   *

Nor doubt, my Emma, but in many an hour
Fancy, who sleeps, shall wake with all her power;
And we shall pass—though not perhaps remain—
To fairy-land, and feel its charm again.

BOOK XVII

THE WIDOW

THE WIDOW ACCEPTS

*   *   *

'The things he offer'd, she must needs confess,
'They were all women's wishes, more or less,
'But were expensive; though a man of sense
'Would by his prudence lighten the expense:
'Prudent he was, but made a sad mistake
'When he proposed her faded face to take;
'And yet, 't is said, there 's beauty that will last
'When the rose withers and the bloom be past.

'One thing displeased her,—that he could suppose
'He might so soon his purposes disclose;
'Yet had she hints of such intent before,
'And would excuse him if he wrote no more:
'What would the world?—and yet she judged them
          fools
'Who let the world's suggestions be their rules:
'What would her friends?—yet in her own affairs
'It was her business to decide, not theirs:
'Adieu! then, sir,' she added; 'thus you find
'The changeless purpose of a steady mind,
'In one now left alone, but to her fate resign'd.

The marriage follow'd.

*   *   *

BOOK XIX

WILLIAM BAILEY

THE RIGHTS OF MAN

*   *   *

'What call you then, my friend, the rights of
    man?'—
'To get his bread,' said William, 'if he can;
'And if he cannot, he must then depend
'Upon a Being he may make his friend.'
'Make!' they replied; and conference had end.

*   *   *

BOOK XXI

SMUGGLERS AND POACHERS

There was a Widow in the village known
To our good Squire, and he had favour shown
By frequent bounty.—She as usual came,
And Richard saw the worn and weary frame,
Pale cheek, and eye subdued, of her whose mind
Was grateful still, and glad a friend to find,
Though to the world long since and all its hopes
    resign'd:
Her easy form, in rustic neatness clad,
Was pleasing still, but she for ever sad.

  'Deep is her grief!' said Richard,—'truly deep,
'And very still, and therefore seems to sleep;
'To borrow simile, to paint her woes,
'Theirs, like the river's motion, seems repose,

'Making no petty murmuring,—settled, slow,
'They never waste, they never overflow.
'Rachel is one of those—for there are some
'Who look for nothing in their days to come,
'No good nor evil, neither hope nor fear,
'Nothing remains or cheerful or severe;
'One day is like the past, the year's sweet prime
'Like the sad fall,—for Rachel heeds not time:
'Nothing remains to agitate her breast,
'Spent is the tempest, and the sky at rest;
'But while it raged her peace its ruin met,
'And now the sun is on her prospects set;—
'Leave her, and let us her distress explore,
'She heeds it not—she has been left before.'

There were two lads call'd Shelley hither brought,
But whence we know not—it was never sought;
Their wandering mother left them, left her name,
And the boys throve and valiant men became:
Handsome, of more than common size, and tall,
And, no one's kindred, seem'd beloved of all:
All seem'd alliance by their deeds to prove,
And loved the youths who could not claim their love.
One was call'd James, the more sedate and grave,
The other Robert—names their neighbours gave;
They both were brave, but Robert loved to run
And meet his danger—James would rather shun
The dangerous trial, but, whenever tried,
He all his spirit to the act applied.

Robert would aid on any man bestow,
James would his man and the occasion know;

For that was quick and prompt—this temperate and
　　slow.
Robert would all things he desired pursue,
James would consider what was best to do;
All spoke of Robert as a man they loved,
And most of James as valued and approved.

　　Both had some learning: Robert his acquired
By quicker parts, and was by praise inspired;
James, as he was in his acquirements slow,
Would learn the worth of what he tried to know.
In fact, this youth was generous—that was just;
The one you loved, the other you would trust:
Yet him you loved you would for truth approve,
And him you trusted you would likewise love.

　　Such were the brothers—James had found his way
To Nether Hall, and there inclined to stay;
He could himself command, and therefore could obey.
He with the keeper took his daily round,
A rival grew, and some unkindness found;
But his superior farm'd! the place was void,
And James guns, dogs, and dignity enjoy'd.

　　Robert had scorn of service; he would be
A slave to no man—happy were the free,
And only they: by such opinions led,
Robert to sundry kinds of trade was bred;
Nor let us wonder if he sometimes made
An active partner in a lawless trade;
Fond of adventure, wanton as the wave,
He loved the danger and the law to brave;
But these were chance-adventures, known to few,—
Not that the hero cared what people knew.

The brothers met not often—When they met,
James talk'd of honest gains and scorn of debt,
Of virtuous labour, of a sober life,
And what with credit would support a wife.

But Robert answer'd,—'How can men advise
'Who to a master let their tongue and eyes?
'Whose words are not their own? whose foot and hand
'Run at a nod, or act upon command?
'Who cannot eat or drink, discourse or play,
'Without requesting others that they may?
'Debt you would shun; but what advice to give,
'Who owe your service every hour you live!
'Let a bell sound, and from your friends you run,
'Although the darling of your heart were one;
'But if the bondage fits you, I resign
'You to your lot—I am content with mine!'

Thus would the Lads their sentiments express,
And part in earnest, part in playfulness;
Till Love, controller of all hearts and eyes,
Breaker of bonds, of friendship's holy ties,
Awakener of new wills and slumbering sympathies,
Began his reign,—till Rachel, meek-eyed maid,
That form, those cheeks, that faultless face display'd,
That child of gracious nature, ever neat
And never fine; a flow'ret simply sweet,
Seeming at least unconscious she was fair;
Meek in her spirit, timid in her air,
And shrinking from his glance if one presumed
To come too near the beauty as it bloom'd.

Robert beheld her in her father's cot
Day after day, and bless'd his happy lot;

He look'd indeed, but he could not offend
By gentle looks—he was her father's friend:
She was accustom'd to that tender look,
And frankly gave the hand he fondly took;
She loved his stories, pleased she heard him play,
Pensive herself, she loved to see him gay,
And if they loved not yet, they were in Love's
    highway.

But Rachel now to womanhood was grown,
And would no more her faith and fondness own;
She call'd her latent prudence to her aid,
And grew observant, cautious, and afraid;
She heard relations of her lover's guile,
And could believe the danger of his smile;
With art insidious rival damsels strove
To show how false his speech, how feign'd his love;
And though her heart another story told,
Her speech grew cautious, and her manner cold.

Rachel had village fame, was fair and tall,
And gain'd a place of credit at the Hall;
Where James beheld her seated in that place,
With a child's meekness, and an angel's face;
Her temper soft, her spirit firm, her words
Simple and few as simple truth affords.

James could but love her,—he at church had seen
The tall, fair maid, had met her on the green,
Admiring, always, nor surprised to find
Her figure often present to his mind;
But now he saw her daily, and the sight
Gave him new pleasure and increased delight.

But James, still prudent and reserved, though sure
The love he felt was love that would endure,
Would wait a while, observing what was fit,
And meet, and right, nor would himself commit;
Then was he flatter'd—James in time became
Rich, both as slayer of the Baron's game
And as protector,—not a female dwelt
In that demesne who had not feign'd or felt
Regard for James; and he from all had praise
Enough a young man's vanity to raise;
With all these pleasures he of course must part,
When Rachel reign'd sole empress of his heart.

Robert was now deprived of that delight
He once experienced in his mistress' sight;
For, though he now his frequent visits paid,
He saw but little of the cautious maid:
The simple common pleasures that he took
Grew dull, and he the wonted haunts forsook;
His flute and song he left, his book and pen,
And sought the meetings of adventurous men;
There was a love-born sadness in his breast,
That wanted stimulus to bring on rest;
These simple pleasures were no more of use,
And danger only could repose produce;
He join'd th' associates in their lawless trade,
And was at length of their profession made.

He saw connected with th' adventurous crew
Those whom he judged were sober men and true;
He found that some, who should the trade prevent,
Gave it by purchase their encouragement;

He found that contracts could be made with those
Who had their pay these dealers to oppose;
And the good ladies whom at church he saw
With looks devout, of reverence and awe,
Could change their feelings as they change their place,
And, whispering, deal for spicery and lace:
And thus the craft and avarice of these
Urged on the youth, and gave his conscience ease.

Him loved the maiden Rachel, fondly loved,
As many a sigh and tear in absence proved,
And many a fear for dangers that she knew,
And many a doubt what one so gay might do:
Of guilt she thought not,—she had often heard
They bought and sold, and nothing wrong appear'd;
Her father's maxim this: she understood
There was some ill,—but he, she knew, was good:
It was a traffic—but was done by night—
If wrong, how trade? why secrecy, if right?
But Robert's conscience, she believed, was pure—
And that he read his Bible she was sure.

James, better taught, in confidence declared
His grief for what his guilty brother dared:
He sigh'd to think how near he was akin
To one reduced by godless men to sin;
Who, being always of the law in dread,
To other crimes were by the danger led—
And crimes with like excuse.—The Smuggler cries,
'What guilt is his who pays for what he buys?'
The Poacher questions, with perverted mind,
'Were not the gifts of Heaven for all design'd?'

This cries, 'I sin not—take not till I pay';—
That, 'My own hand brought down my proper
          prey':—
And while to such fond arguments they cling,
How fear they God? how honour they the king?
Such men associate, and each other aid,
Till all are guilty, rash, and desperate made;
Till to some lawless deed the wretches fly,
And in the act, or for the acting, die.

The maid was frighten'd,—but, if this was true,
Robert for certain no such danger knew;
He always pray'd ere he a trip began,
And was too happy for a wicked man:
How could a creature, who was always gay,
So kind to all men, so disposed to pray,—
How could he give his heart to such an evil way?
Yet she had fears,—for she could not believe
That James could lie, or purpose to deceive;
But still she found, though not without respect
For one so good, she must the man reject;
For, simple though she was, full well she knew
What this strong friendship led him to pursue;
And, let the man be honest as the light,
Love warps the mind a little from the right;
And she proposed, against the trying day,
What in the trial she should think and say.

And now, their love avow'd, in both arose
Fear and disdain,—the orphan pair were foes.

Robert, more generous of the two, avow'd
His scorn, defiance, and contempt aloud.

James talk'd of pity in a softer tone,
To Rachel speaking, and with her alone:
He knew full well, he said, to what must come
His wretched brother, what would be his doom:
Thus he her bosom fenced with dread about;
But love he could not with his skill drive out.
Still he effected something,—and that skill
Made the love wretched, though it could not kill;
And Robert fail'd, though much he tried, to prove
He had no guilt—she granted he had love.

Thus they proceeded, till a winter came,
When the stern keeper told of stolen game:
Throughout the woods the poaching dogs had been,
And from him nothing should the robbers screen,
From him and law,—he would all hazards run,
Nor spare a poacher, were his brother one,—
Love, favour, interest, tie of blood should fail,
Till vengeance bore him bleeding to the jail.

Poor Rachel shudder'd,—smuggling she could name
Without confusion, for she felt not shame;
But poachers were her terror, and a wood
Which they frequented had been mark'd by blood;
And though she thought her Robert was secure
In better thoughts, yet could she not be sure.

James now was urgent,—it would break his heart
With hope, with her, and with such views to part,
When one so wicked would her hand possess,
And he a brother!—that was his distress,
And must be hers.—She heard him, and she sigh'd,
Looking in doubt,—but nothing she replied.

There was a generous feeling in her mind,
That told her this was neither good nor kind:
James caused her terror, but he did no more—
Her love was now as it had been before.

Their traffic fail'd—and the adventurous crew
No more their profitless attempts renew:
Dig they will not, and beg they might in vain,
Had they not pride, and what can then remain?

Now was the game destroy'd, and not a hare
Escaped at least the danger of the snare;
Woods of their feather'd beauty were bereft,
The beauteous victims of the silent theft;
The well-known shops received a large supply,
That they who could not kill at least might buy.

James was enraged, enraged his lord, and both
Confirm'd their threatening with a vengeful oath:
Fresh aid was sought,—and nightly on the lands
Walk'd on their watch the strong, determined bands:
Pardon was offer'd, and a promised pay,
To him who would the desperate gang betray.
Nor fail'd the measure,—on a certain night
A few were seized—the rest escaped by flight;
Yet they resisted boldly ere they fled,
And blows were dealt around, and blood was shed;
Two groaning helpers on the earth were laid,
When more arrived the lawful cause to aid;
Then four determined men were seized and bound,
And Robert in this desperate number found:
In prison fetter'd, he deplored his fate,
And cursed the folly he perceived too late.

205

James was a favourite with his lord,—the zeal
He show'd was such as masters ever feel:
If he for vengeance on a culprit cried,
Or if for mercy, still his lord complied;
And now, 't was said, he will for mercy plead,
For his own brother's was the guilty deed:
True, the hurt man is in a mending way,
But must be crippled to his dying day.

Now James had vow'd the law should take its
    course,
He would not stay it, if he did not force;
He could his witness, if he pleased, withdraw,
Or he could arm with certain death the law:
This he attested to the maid, and true,
If this he could not, yet he much could do.

How suffer'd then that maid!—no thought she had,
No view of days to come, that was not sad;
As sad as life with all its hopes resign'd,
As sad as aught but guilt can make mankind.

With bitter grief the pleasure she review'd
Of early hope, with innocence pursued,
When she began to love, and he was fond and good.
He now must die, she heard from every tongue—
Die, and so thoughtless! perish, and so young!
Brave, kind, and generous, tender, constant, true—
And he must die—'Then will I perish too!'

A thousand acts in every age will prove
Women are valiant in a cause they love;
If fate the favour'd swain in danger place,
They heed not danger—perils they embrace;

206

They dare the world's contempt, they brave their
　　name's disgrace;
They on the ocean meet its wild alarms,
They search the dungeon with extended arms;
The utmost trial of their faith they prove,
And yield the lover to assert their love.

　　James knew his power—his feelings were not nice—
Mercy he sold, and she must pay the price:
If his good lord forbore to urge their fate,
And he the utmost of their guilt to state,
The felons might their forfeit lives redeem,
And in their country's cause regain esteem;
But never more that man, whom he had shame
To call his brother, must she see or name.

　　Rachel was meek, but she had firmness too,
And reason'd much on what she ought to do:
In Robert's place, she knew what she should choose—
But life was not the thing she fear'd to lose:
She knew that she could not their contract break,
Nor for her life a new engagement make;
But he was man, and guilty,—death so near
Might not to his as to her mind appear;
And he might wish, to spare that forfeit life,
The maid he loved might be his brother's wife,
Although that brother was his bitter foe,
And he must all the sweets of life forego.

　　This would she try,—intent on this alone,
She could assume a calm and settled tone:
She spake with firmness,—'I will Robert see,
'Know what he wishes, and what I must be';

For James had now discover'd to the maid
His inmost heart, and how he must be paid,
If he his lord would soften, and would hide
The facts that must the culprit's fate decide.
'Go not', he said,—for she her full intent
Proclaim'd—to go she purposed, and she went:
She took a guide, and went with purpose stern
The secret wishes of her friend to learn.

She saw him fetter'd, full of grief, alone,
Still as the dead, and he suppress'd a groan
At her appearance.—Now she pray'd for strength;
And the sad couple could converse at length.
It was a scene that shook her to repeat,—
Life fought with love, both powerful, and both sweet.

'Wilt thou die, Robert, or preserve thy life?
'Shall I be thine own maid, or James's wife?'

'His wife!—No!—never will I thee resign—
'No, Rachel no!'—'Then am I ever thine:
'I know thee rash and guilty,—but to thee
'I pledged my vow, and thine will ever be.
'Yet think again,—the life that God has lent
'Is thine, but not to cast away—consent,
'If 't is thy wish; for this I made my way
'To thy distress—command, and I obey.'

'Perhaps my brother may have gain'd thy heart?'
'Then why this visit, if I wish'd to part?
'Was it—ah, man ungrateful!—wise to make
'Effort like this, to hazard for thy sake
'A spotless reputation, and to be
'A suppliant to that stern man for thee!

208

'But I forgive,—thy spirit has been tried,
'And thou art weak, but still thou must decide.

  'I ask'd thy brother James, "Wouldst thou command,
'Without the loving heart, the obedient hand?"
'I ask thee, Robert, lover, canst thou part
'With this poor hand, when master of the heart?—
'He answer'd, "Yes!"—I tarry thy reply,
'Resign'd with him to live, content with thee to die.'

  Assured of this, with spirits low and tame,
Here life so purchased—there a death of shame;
Death once his merriment, but now his dread,
And he with terror thought upon the dead:
'O! sure 't is better to endure the care
'And pain of life, than go we know not where:—
'And is there not the dreaded hell for sin,
'Or is it only this I feel within?
'That, if it lasted, no man would sustain,
'But would by any change relieve the pain:
'Forgive me, love! it is a loathsome thing
'To live not thine; but still this dreaded sting
'Of death torments me,—I to nature cling.
'Go, and be his—but love him not, be sure—
'Go, love him not,—and I will life endure:
'He too, is mortal!'—Rachel deeply sigh'd,
But would no more converse: she had complied,
And was no longer free—she was his brother's bride.

  'Farewell!' she said, with kindness, but not fond,
Feeling the pressure of the recent bond,
And put her tenderness apart to give
Advice to one who so desired to live:

She then departed, join'd the attending guide,
Reflected—wept—was sad—was satisfied.

James on her worth and virtue could depend,—
He listen'd gladly to her story's end:
Again he promised Robert's life to save,
And claim'd the hand that she in payment gave.

Robert, when death no longer was in view,
Scorn'd what was done, but could not this undo:
The day appointed for the trial near
He view'd with shame, and not unmix'd with fear:
James might deceive him; and, if not, the schemes
Of men may fail.—'Can I depend on James?'

He might; for now the grievous price was paid—
James to the altar led the victim maid,
And gave the trembling girl his faithful word
For Robert's safety, and so gave my lord.

But this, and all the promise hope could give,
Gilded not life,—it was not joy to live;
There was no smile in Rachel, nothing gay,
The hours pass'd off, but never danced away.
When drew the gloomy day for trial near,
There came a note to Robert,—'Banish fear!'

He knew whence safety came,—his terror fled,
But rage and vengeance fill'd his soul instead.

A stronger fear in his companions rose—
The day of trial on their hopes might close:
They had no brothers, none to intercede
For them, their friends suspected, and in need;

Scatter'd, they judged, and could unite no more,—
Not so,—they then were at the prison door.

For some had met who sought the haunts they loved,
And were to pity and to vengeance moved:
Their fellows perish? and they see their fall?—
Why not attempt the steep but guardless wall?

Attempt was made, his part assign'd each man,
And they succeeded in the desperate plan;
In truth, a purposed mercy smoothed their way,
But that they knew not—all triumphant they.
Safe in their well-known haunts, they all prepared
To plan anew, and show how much they dared.

With joy the troubled heart of Robert beat,
For life was his, and liberty was sweet;
He look'd around in freedom—in delight?
O! no—his Rachel was another's right!
'Right!—has he then preserved me in the day
'Of my distress?—He has the lovely pay!
'But I no freedom at the slave's request,—
'The price I paid shall then be repossess'd!
'Alas! her virtue and the law prevent,
'Force cannot be, and she will not consent;
'But were that brother gone!—A brother? No!
'A circumventor!—and the wretch shall go!
'Yet not this hand—How shifts about my mind,
'Ungovern'd, guideless, drifting in the wind!
'And I am all a tempest, whirl'd around
'By dreadful thoughts, that fright me and confound.
'I would I saw him on the earth laid low!
'I wish the fate, but must not give the blow!'

So thinks a man when thoughtful; he prefers
A life of peace till man his anger stirs,
Then all the efforts of his reason cease,
And he forgets how pleasant was that peace;
Till the wild passions what they seek obtain,
And then he sinks into his calm again.

Now met the lawless clan,—in secret met,
And down at their convivial board were set;
The plans in view to past adventures led,
And the past conflicts present anger bred;
They sigh'd for pleasures gone, they groan'd for
    heroes dead:
Their ancient stores were rifled,—strong desires
Awaked, and wine rekindled latent fires.

It was a night such bold desires to move,
Strong winds and wintry torrents fill'd the grove;
The crackling boughs that in the forest fell,
The cawing rooks, the cur's affrighten'd yell,
The scenes above the wood, the floods below,
Were mix'd, and none the single sound could know;
'Loud blow the blasts', they cried, 'and call us as
    they blow.'

In such a night—and then the heroes told
What had been done in better times of old;
How they had conquer'd all opposed to them,
By force in part, in part by stratagem;
And as the tales inflamed the fiery crew,
What had been done they then prepared to do;
''T is a last night!' they said—the angry blast
And roaring floods seem'd answering, ''T is a last!'

James knew they met, for he had spies about,
Grave, sober men, whom none presumed to doubt!
For if suspected, they had soon been tried
Where fears are evidence, and doubts decide:
But these escaped.—Now James companions took,
Sturdy and bold, with terror-stirring look:
He had before, by informations led,
Left the afflicted partner of his bed;
Awaked his men, and through plantations wide,
Deep woods, and trackless ling, had been their guide:
And then return'd to wake the pitying wife,
And hear her tender terrors for his life.

But in this night a sure informer came,—
They were assembled who attack'd his game;
Who more than once had through the park made way,
And slain the dappled breed, or vow'd to slay;
The trembling spy had heard the solemn vow,
And need and vengeance both inspired them now.

The keeper early had retired to rest
For brief repose; sad thoughts his mind possess'd;
In his short sleep he started from his bed,
And ask'd in fancy's terror, 'Is he dead?'
There was a call below, when James awoke,
Rose from his bed, and arms to aid him took,
Not all defensive!—there his helpers stood,
Arm'd like himself, and hastening to the wood.

'Why this?' he said; for Rachel pour'd her tears
Profuse, that spoke involuntary fears:
'Sleep, that so early thou for us mayst wake,
'And we our comforts in return may take;

213

'Sleep, and farewell!' he said, and took his way,
And the sad wife in neither could obey;
She slept not nor well fared, but restless dwelt
On her past life, and past afflictions felt:
The man she loved, the brother and the foe
Of him she married!—It had wrought her woe;
Not that she loved, but pitied, and that now
Was, so she fear'd, infringement of her vow:
James too was civil, though she must confess
That his was not her kind of happiness:
That he would shoot the man who shot a hare,
Was what her timid conscience could not bear;
But still she loved him—wonder'd where he stray'd
In this loud night, and if he were afraid.

More than one hour she thought, and, dropping then
In sudden sleep, cried loudly, 'Spare him, men!
'And do no murder!'—then awaked she rose,
And thought no more of trying for repose.

'T was past the dead of night, when every sound
That nature mingles might be heard around;
But none from man,—man's feeble voice was hush'd,
Where rivers swelling roar'd, and woods were crush'd;
Hurried by these, the wife could sit no more,
But must the terrors of the night explore.

Softly she left her door, her garden gate,
And seem'd as then committed to her fate:
To every horrid thought and doubt a prey,
She hurried on, already lost her way:
Oft as she glided on in that sad night,
She stopp'd to listen, and she look'd for light;

An hour she wander'd, and was still to learn
Aught of her husband's safety or return:
A sudden break of heavy clouds could show
A place she knew not, but she strove to know:
Still further on she crept with trembling feet,
With hope a friend, with fear a foe to meet;
And there was something fearful in the sight
And in the sound of what appear'd to-night;
For now, of night and nervous terror bred,
Arose a strong and superstitious dread;
She heard strange noises, and the shapes she saw
Of fancied beings bound her soul in awe.

The moon was risen, and she sometimes shone
Through thick white clouds, that flew tumultuous on,
Passing beneath her with an eagle's speed,
That her soft light imprison'd and then freed:
The fitful glimmering through the hedge-row green
Gave a strange beauty to the changing scene;
And roaring winds and rushing waters lent
Their mingled voice that to the spirit went.

To these she listen'd; but new sounds were heard,
And sight more startling to her soul appear'd;
There were low lengthen'd tones with sobs between,
And near at hand, but nothing yet was seen,
She hurried on, and 'Who is there?' she cried,—
'A dying wretch!' was from the earth replied.

It was her lover—was the man she gave
The price she paid, himself from death to save;
With whom, expiring, she must kneel and pray,

While the soul flitted from the shivering clay
That press'd the dewy ground, and bled its life away!
This was the part that duty bade her take,
Instant and ere her feelings were awake;
But now they waked to anguish: there came then,
Hurrying with lights, loud-speaking, eager men.

   'And here, my lord, we met—And who is here?
'The keeper's wife!—Ah! woman, go not near!
'There lies the man that was the head of all—
'See, in his temples went the fatal ball!
'And James that instant, who was then our guide,
'Felt in his heart the adverse shot, and died!
'It was a sudden meeting, and the light
'Of a dull moon made indistinct our fight;
'He foremost fell!—But see, the woman creeps
'Like a lost thing, that wanders as she sleeps.
'See, here her husband's body—but she knows
'That other dead, and that her action shows.
'Rachel! why look you at your mortal foe?—
'She does not hear us—Whither will she go?'

   Now, more attentive, on the dead they gazed,
And they were brothers: sorrowing and amazed,
On all a momentary silence came,
A common softness, and a moral shame.

   'Seized you the poachers?' said my lord.—'They fled,
'And we pursued not—one of them was dead,
'And one of us: they hurried through the wood,
'Two lives were gone, and we no more pursued.
'Two lives of men, of valiant brothers, lost!
'Enough, my lord, do hares and pheasants cost!'

So many thought, and there is found a heart
To dwell upon the deaths on either part;
Since this their morals have been more correct,
The cruel spirit in the place is check'd;
His lordship holds not in such sacred care,
Nor takes such dreadful vengeance for a hare;
The smugglers fear, the poacher stands in awe
Of Heaven's own act, and reverence the law;
There was, there is, a terror in the place
That operates on man's offending race;
Such acts will stamp their moral on the soul,
And, while the bad they threaten and control,
Will to the pious and the humble say,
Yours is the right, the safe, the certain way;
'T is wisdom to be good, 't is virtue to obey.

So Rachel thinks, the pure, the good, the meek,
Whose outward acts the inward purpose speak;
As men will children at their sports behold,
And smile to see them, though unmoved and cold,
Smile at the recollected games, and then
Depart and mix in the affairs of men:
So Rachel looks upon the world, and sees
It cannot longer pain her, longer please,
But just detain the passing thought, or cause
A gentle smile of pity or applause;
And then the recollected soul repairs
Her slumbering hope, and heeds her own affairs.

TALE V

VILLARS

THE PRISON FOR THE GUILTY WIFE

*   *   *

VILLARS long since, as he indulged his spleen
By lonely travel on the coast, had seen
A large old mansion suffer'd to decay
In some law-strife, and slowly drop away.
Dark elms around the constant herons bred,
Those the marsh dykes, the neighbouring ocean fed;
Rocks near the coast no shipping would allow,
And stubborn heath around forbade the plough;
Dull must the scene have been in years of old,
But now was wildly dismal to behold—
One level sadness! marsh, and heath, and sea,
And, save these high dark elms, nor plant nor tree.

In this bleak ruin Villars found a room,
Square, small, and lofty—seat of grief and gloom:
A sloping skylight on the white wall threw,
When the sun set, a melancholy hue;
The hall of Vathek has a room so bare,
So small, so sad, so form'd to nourish care.

*   *   *

THE FAREWELL AND RETURN

TWENTY YEARS AFTER

*   *   *

The very place is alter'd. What I left
Seems of its space and dignity bereft:
The streets are narrow, and the buildings mean;
Did I, or Fancy, leave them broad and clean?
The ancient church, in which I felt a pride,
As struck by magic, is but half as wide;
The tower is shorter, the sonorous bell
Tells not the hour as it was wont to tell;
The market dwindles, every shop and stall
Sinks in my view; there 's littleness in all.
Mine is the error; prepossess'd I see;
And all the change I mourn is change in me.

One object only is the same; the sight
Of the wide Ocean by the moon's pale light,
With her long ray of glory, that we mark
On the wild waves when all beside is dark:
This is the work of Nature, and the eye
In vain the boundless prospect would descry;
What mocks our view cannot contracted be;
We cannot lessen what we cannot see.

*   *   *

THE ANCIENT MANSION

* * *

Here I behold no puny works of art,
None give me reasons why these views impart
Such charm to fill the mind, such joy to swell the heart.
These very pinnacles, and turrets small,
And windows dim, have beauty in them all.
How stately stand yon pines upon the hill,
How soft the murmurs of that living rill!
And o'er the park's tall paling, scarcely higher,
Peeps the low Church and shows the modest spire.
Unnumber'd violets on those banks appear,
And all the first-born beauties of the year.
The grey-green blossoms of the willows bring
The large wild bees upon the labouring wing;
Then comes the Summer with augmented pride,
Whose pure small streams along the valleys glide:
Her richer Flora their brief charms display,
And, as the fruit advances, fall away.
Then shall th' autumnal yellow clothe the leaf,
What time the reaper binds the burden'd sheaf:
Then silent groves denote the dying year,
The morning frost, and noontide gossamer;
And all be silent in the scene around,
All save the distant sea's uncertain sound.

* * *

And then the wintry winds begin to blow,
Then fall the flaky stars of gathering snow,

When on the thorn the ripening sloe, yet blue,
Takes the bright varnish of the morning dew;
The aged moss grows brittle on the pale,
The dry boughs splinter in the windy gale,
And every changing season of the year
Stamps on the scene its English character.

*   *   *

TALE XIII

THE DEAN'S LADY

*   *   *

Her hungry mind on every subject feeds;
She Adam Smith and Dugald Stewart reads;
Locke entertains her, and she wonders why
His famous Essay is consider'd dry.
For her amusement in her vacant hours
Are earths and rocks and animals and flowers:
She could the farmer at his work assist,
A systematic agriculturist.
Some men, indeed, would curb the female mind,
Nor let us see that they themselves are blind;
But—thank our stars!—the liberal times allow
That all may think, and men have rivals now.

Miranda deems all knowledge might be gain'd—
'But she is idle, nor has much attain'd;
'Men are in her deceived: she knows at most
'A few light matters, for she scorns to boast:
'Her mathematic studies she resign'd—
'They did not suit the genius of her mind.

'She thought indeed the higher parts sublime,
'But then they took a monstrous deal of time!'

Frequent and full the letters she delights
To read in part; she names not him who writes—
But here and there a precious sentence shows,
Telling what literary debts she owes.
Works, yet unprinted, for her judgment come;
'Alas!' she cries, 'and I must seal their doom.
'Sworn to be just, the judgment gives me pain—
'Ah! why must truth be told, or man be vain?'

Much she has written, and still deigns to write,
But not an effort yet must see the light.
'Cruel!' her friends exclaim; 'unkind, unjust!'
But, no! the envious mass she will not trust;
Content to hear that fame is due to her,
Which on her works the world might not confer—
Content with loud applauses while she lives;
Unfelt the pain the cruel critic gives.

* * *

TALE XIV

THE WIFE AND WIDOW

THE MANAGING WIFE

* * *

Nor watch'd she less the Husband's weaker soul,
But learn'd to lead him who abhorr'd control,
Who thought a nursery, next a kitchen, best
To women suited, and she acquiesced;

She only begg'd to rule in small affairs,
And ease her wedded lord of common cares,
Till he at length thought every care was small,
Beneath his notice, and she had them all.
He on his throne the lawful monarch sate,
And she was by—the minister of state:
He gave assent, and he required no more,
But sign'd the act that she decreed before.

*   *   *

TALE XV

BELINDA WATERS

BEFORE MARRIAGE

*   *   *

Behold her now! she on her sofa looks
O'er half a shelf of circulating books.
This she admired, but she forgets the name,
And reads again another, or the same.

*   *   *

AFTER

*   *   *

Yes! she is married; though she waited long,
Not from a prudent fear of choosing wrong,
But want of choice.—She took a surgeon's mate,
With his half-pay, that was his whole estate.

Fled is the charming bloom that nature spread
Upon her cheek, the pure, the rosy red—

This, and the look serene, the calm, kind look,
    are fled.
Sorrow and sadness now the place possess,
And the pale cast of anxious fretfulness.

She *wonders* much—as, why they live so ill,—
Why the rude butcher brings his weekly bill,—
She wonders why that baker will not trust,—
And says, most truly says,—'Indeed, he must.'
She wonders where her former friends are gone,—
And thus, from day to day, she wonders on.

Howe'er she can,—she dresses gaily yet,
And then she wonders how they came in debt.
Her husband loves her, and in accent mild
Answers, and treats her like a fretted child;
But when he, ruffled, makes severe replies,
And seems unhappy, then she pouts and cries
'She wonders when she 'll die!'—She faints, but
    never dies.

'How well my father lived!' she says.—'How well,
'My dear, your father's creditors could tell!'

*   * *   *

APPENDIX

FROM THE PARODY OF CRABBE BY JAMES SMITH IN
REJECTED ADDRESSES (1812)

THE THEATRE

Interior of a theatre described—Pit gradually fills—The Check-taker—Pit
full—The Orchestra tuned—One Fiddler rather dilatory—Is reproved—and
repents—Evolutions of a Play-bill—Its final settlement on the spikes—The
Gods taken to task—and why—Motley Group of Play-goers—Holywell
Street, St Pancras—Emanuel Jennings binds his son apprentice—not in
London—and why—Episode of the Hat.

'T is sweet to view, from half-past five to six,
Our long wax-candles, with short cotton wicks,
Touch'd by the lamp-lighter's Promethean art,
Start into light and make the lighter start;
To see red Phoebus through the gallery-pane
Tinge with his beam the beams of Drury Lane;
While gradual parties fill our widen'd pit,
And gape, and gaze, and wonder, ere they sit.

At first, while vacant seats give choice and ease,
Distant or near, they settle where they please;
But when the multitude contracts the span,
And seats are rare, they settle where they can.

Now the full benches to late-comers doom
No room for standing, miscall'd *standing room.*

Hark! the check-taker moody silence breaks,
And bawling 'Pit full!' gives the check he takes;
Yet onward still the gathering numbers cram,
Contending crowders shout the frequent damn,
And all is bustle, squeeze, row, jabbering, and jam.

See to their desks Apollo's sons repair—
Swift rides the rosin o'er the horse's hair!
In unison their various tones to tune,
Murmurs the hautboy, growls the hoarse bassoon;
In soft vibration sighs the whispering lute,
Tang goes the harpsichord, too-too the flute,
Brays the loud trumpet, squeaks the fiddle sharp,
Winds the French horn and twangs the tinkling
        harp;
Till, like great Jove, the leader, figuring in,
Attunes to order the chaotic din.
Now all seems hush'd—but, no, one fiddle will
Give, half-ashamed, a tiny flourish still.
Foil'd in his crash, the leader of the clan
Reproves with frowns the dilatory man:
Then on his candlestick thrice taps his bow,
Nods a new signal, and away they go.

      *   *   *

John Richard William Alexander Dwyer
Was footman to Justinian Stubbs, Esquire;
But when John Dwyer listed in the Blues,
Emanuel Jennings polish'd Stubbs's shoes.
Emanuel Jennings brought his youngest boy
Up as a corn-cutter—a safe employ;
In Holywell Street, St Pancras, he was bred
(At number twenty-seven, it is said),
Facing the pump, and near the Granby's Head:
He would have bound him to some shop in town,
But with a premium he could not come down.
Pat was the urchin's name—a red-hair'd youth,
Fonder of purl and skittle-grounds than truth.

Silence, ye gods! to keep your tongues in awe,
The Muse shall tell an accident she saw.

Pat Jennings in the upper gallery sat,
But, leaning forward, Jennings lost his hat:
Down from the gallery the beaver flew,
And spurn'd the one to settle in the two.
How shall he act? Pay at the gallery-door
Two shillings for what cost, when new, but four?
Or till half-price, to save his shilling, wait,
And gain his hat again at half-past eight?
Now, while his fears anticipate a thief,
John Mullins whispers, 'Take my handkerchief.'
'Thank you,' cries Pat; 'but one won't make a line.'
'Take mine,' cried Wilson; and cried Stokes, 'Take
      mine.'
A motley cable soon Pat Jennings ties,
Where Spitalfields with real India vies.
Like Iris' bow, down darts the painted clue,
Starr'd, striped, and spotted, yellow, red, and blue,
Old calico, torn silk, and muslin new.
George Green below, with palpitating hand,
Loops the last 'kerchief to the beaver's band—
Upsoars the prize! The youth, with joy unfeign'd,
Regain'd the felt, and felt what he regain'd;
While to the applauding galleries grateful Pat
Made a low bow, and touch'd the ransom'd hat.

CAMBRIDGE: PRINTED BY W. LEWIS, M.A., AT THE UNIVERSITY PRESS